Reflective Practice in Action

Reflective Practice in Action
80 Reflection Breaks for Busy Teachers

Thomas S. C. Farrell

CORWIN PRESS
A Sage Publications Company
Thousand Oaks, California

For information:

Corwin Press
A Sage Publications Company
2455 Teller Road
Thousand Oaks, California 91320
www.corwinpress.com

Sage Publications Ltd.
6 Bonhill Street
London EC2A 4PU
United Kingdom

Sage Publications India Pvt. Ltd.
B-42, Panchsheel Enclave
Post Box 4109
New Delhi 110 017 India

Printed in the United States of America

Library of Congress Cataloging-in-Publication Data

Farrell, Thomas S. C. (Thomas Sylvester Charles) Reflective practice in action: 80 reflection breaks for busy teachers / by Thomas S. C. Farrell.
    p. cm.
Includes bibliographical references and index.
ISBN 0-7619-3163-5 (Cloth)
ISBN 0-7619-3164-3 (Paper)
    1. Reflective teaching. 2. Teacher effectiveness. I. Title.
LB1027.F28 2004
371.102—dc22

                                                    2003017022
This book is printed on acid-free paper.

03   04   05   06   07   10   9   8   7   6   5   4   3   2   1

Acquisitions Editor:	Faye Zucker
Editorial Assistant:	Stacy Wagner
Production Editor:	Julia Parnell
Copy Editor:	Marilyn Power Scott
Proofreader:	Kathrine Pollock
Typesetter:	C&M Digitals (P) Ltd.
Indexer:	Sylvia Coates
Cover Designer:	Tracy E. Miller
Graphic Designer:	Lisa Miller

Contents

Preface

*R**eflective Practice in Action* is designed to serve teachers interested in improving their professional development. It can be used as a textbook for inservice teacher development courses as well as for teacher preparation courses. The book can also be used as a source book for school principals and administrators who want to encourage their teachers to think reflectively about their work.

I strongly believe that teachers should reflect on their work, and this book exists to help them do just that. As reflective practitioners, they can draw meaning from the study of their behaviors and methods inside of the classroom, with the intent to change for the better. The real value of reflection is in separating thought and emotion from the teaching event. Teachers can use this book as a mirror to help them see how their backgrounds have influenced them, who they are now, and where they intend to go in their practice. Reflective teachers have choices, and reflection is only half of the equation; the other half is action. Once teachers come to understand the how and why of what they do and have done, they can then take steps that will carry them along the path to better teaching.

Each chapter in the book attempts to help teachers uncover aspects of their work that may otherwise remain at the tacit level. To save time, teachers may choose to start reflecting at any point in the book and within any chapter. If teachers want to get a good grounding in reflective practice, they can read the first four chapters, which outline the origins and ideas behind reflective practice. Those who want to get down to reflecting immediately may want to begin with Chapter 5, which outlines the model of reflective practice on which many of the Reflection Breaks are based.

Reflective Practice in Action offers busy and dedicated teachers practical suggestions to tackle their professional development needs.

These Reflection Breaks will, I hope, enable teachers to use the insights generated by these activities to create and implement new methods that will make them more effective teachers in their classrooms.

Acknowledgments

This book resulted from my personal reflections as a foreign language teacher over the past twenty-four years. However, it would not have been possible without the help and guidance of many people I encountered along the way. I am particularly grateful to Jerry Gebhard for his encouragement when I first started formalizing reflections on my work. He showed me the true value of exploring our teaching and how this exploration can lead to greater awareness.

Others who have influenced some of my thoughts on reflective practice are Dan Tannacito, Jack Richards, George Jacobs, and David Hayes. I am also grateful to the Singapore Tertiary English Teachers' Society for inviting me to give workshops on reflective practice, in which I developed many of the reflection breaks outlined in this book.

I would also like to thank various colleagues at the National Institute of Education, Singapore, for their support; my wife, Mija, who gently teaches me the value of reflection; and my two daughters, Sarah and Ann, who stimulate me to reflect continuously. Last, a special thanks to Faye Zucker, Executive Editor at Corwin Press, without whose guidance and encouragement this book would not have been possible, and to Stacy Wagner, whose insightful and skillful editing helped shape the manuscript into a more readable and coherent text.

Corwin Press thanks the following reviewers for their contributions to this work:

Scott Abrams, Bend, OR

William Fitzhugh, Reisterstown, MD

George Jacobs, Singapore

Angela Peery, Lady's Island, SC

Linda Sidoti, Albany, NY

William A. Sommers, Edina, MN

Germaine Taggart, Hays, KS

Jennifer York-Barr, Minneapolis, MN

Lawrence Zwier, East Lansing, MI

About the Author

Thomas S. C. Farrell teaches in the Division of English Language & Literature at the National Institute of Education, Nanyang Technological University, Singapore. He received his BComm and HDipEd from University College Dublin, Ireland; his MsEd from the University of Southern California, USA; and his PhD in Rhetoric and Linguistics from Indiana University of Pennsylvania, USA. As a constructivist teacher-educator, his professional interests include reflective teaching, language teacher education and development, and teacher beliefs and teaching methodology. He has published widely in these areas in such journals as *Teaching & Teacher Education, Journal of Education in Teaching, The Teacher Trainer System,* and *English Language Teaching Journal.*

CHAPTER ONE

Introduction to Reflective Practice

A teacher's day never really ends. Wouldn't you agree? In addition to performing the primary responsibility of teaching, many teachers would no doubt like to have the time to sit down and think about what they do inside and outside their classrooms, to catch their breath. They may also feel that they do not have the time to devote to reflecting on their work beyond the fleeting thought of, "Oh, that class went well," or "The students were totally tuned out today." It would be wonderful if administrators recognized the need for teachers to reflect on their work by freeing up some time for that purpose, but unfortunately, that's not the present reality.

Reflective Practice in Action: 80 Reflection Breaks for Busy Teachers can help teachers make the best use of their time before, during, and after class if they want to reflect on their work. The book offers questions and strategies, in the form of Reflection Breaks, on all areas of teaching and learning, to be used according to each teacher's preference. Each Reflection Break has a title for easy reference and is either jargon free or explained in detail.

WHAT REFLECTION BREAKS OFFER

Reflective Practice in Action: 80 Reflection Breaks for Busy Teachers offers a systematic method—so that teachers can reflect at their own paces and at whatever levels they want. If desired, they can go directly to each Reflection Break without reading the surrounding explanation or theory. They can dip into the book at any place or time and think about the questions posed about their work. The explanations can always be read at a later time for deeper reflection. For example, a busy teacher may want to start a teaching journal during the semester. In this case, the teacher can just go straight to Chapter 8 and read the Reflection Breaks about journal writing. Later, when the teacher has finished teaching and has begun reflecting on journal entries, he or she may want to read Chapters 1 through 5 for a more detailed understanding of reflective practice.

One of the main premises of this book is that reflection is crucial for teachers to avoid burnout. I also hope that teachers will become more aware of their practices and more confident and informed decision makers as a result of using this book.

Reflective Practice in Action: 80 Reflection Breaks for Busy Teachers is mainly intended for practicing teachers and teachers enrolled in inservice programs, and it can also be used by beginning and student teachers. Its focus is reflecting on practice so that busy teachers can understand, implement, and enhance reflection in their teaching lives. Educational administrators can also use this book to reflect on their personal stances and understanding of teacher development and reflective practice and hence to encourage their teachers to use the book as part of their professional development.

Structure of the Book

Each chapter is short and to the point. Chapter 1 offers an introduction to the book as a whole. Chapter 2 lays out the benefits of engaging in reflective practice, setting the Reflection Breaks in motion. Chapter 3 outlines various approaches to reflective practice through time. Chapter 4 attempts to define reflective practice and discusses the different levels of reflection. Chapter 5 gives an overall framework to reflective practice for educators by offering a five-component model of reflective practice:

- Providing opportunities to reflect (the main component)
- Building in some ground rules to the process and into each activity

- Making provisions for four different kinds of time: individual, activity, development, and period of reflection
- Providing external input for enriched reflection
- Providing for low affective states

Chapters 6 through 9 detail four activities that can promote reflective practice: group discussions (Chapter 6), classroom observation (Chapter 7), journal writing (Chapter 8), and maintaining a teaching portfolio (Chapter 9). Chapter 10 offers teachers four additional activities they can use to aid reflection in their teaching lives.

Reflective Practice in Action: 80 Reflection Breaks for Busy Teachers is intended for all teachers regardless of the subjects they teach. Each Reflection Break has been tested in seminars and workshops conducted by me with practicing teachers in the United States, the United Kingdom, and other international settings.

If you use the Reflection Breaks in each chapter, I guarantee that you will become more aware of who you are as a teacher and of what informs your practice. I hope that this book enables you to have an exciting reflective journey and that you become a more reflective teacher as a result. You will certainly become a more informed decision maker, and your students can only benefit as a result of your increased level of awareness.

Now, you can begin with the first Reflection Break, taking stock of your development as a teacher thus far and analyzing the results.

**Reflection Break 1
Taking Stock**

Reflect on yourself as a teacher as a starting point on your reflective journey:

- Do you enjoy going into school each morning?
- Do you find teaching exciting and challenging?
- Do you think of teaching as a job or a profession?
- What is the best aspect of your life as a teacher?
- What is the worst aspect of your life as a teacher?

(Continued)

(Continued)

- Do you spend much time thinking about new ideas for teaching your classes?
- Do you ever discuss teaching with your colleagues in the staff room?
- Do you ever ask your peers to watch you teach and later comment on your lessons?
- Are there things you would like to change about your teaching? If so, do you believe that you can change them?
- What have you learned about yourself as a teacher so far?

Now you have begun. Continue your reflective journey through the various chapters in *Reflective Practice in Action*.

CHAPTER TWO

Why Reflect?

W hy should teachers bother to reflect on their work? Many teachers are already overburdened with so many demands on their time outside of the classroom that they really have no room to entertain the idea of reflecting on their teaching. In many countries today there seem to be growing demands on teachers (e.g., the various recent mandates imposed at local and state levels in the United States) to standardize education programs so that students will be able to pass standardized tests. Often, these educational reforms have been authorized (some would say imposed) without input from the teachers who must implement them. Consequently, some teachers have experienced feelings of alienation and isolation because they have been asked to implement changes they have had no part in shaping. Teachers may see themselves as mere technicians executing programs that have been prepackaged and prescribed by others (Nieto, Gordon, & Yearwood, 2002). It is understandable that many teachers feel a sense of helplessness about their situations and roles in an education system perceived to be impersonal.

Though the future of the educational system may seem dire, teachers really can influence their practices much more that they think. As "transformative intellectuals" (Nieto et al., 2002, p. 345) who attempt to reflect on and influence their work, teachers can proactively start to take control of their working lives. As such, they become more empowered decision makers, engaging in systematic reflections of their work by thinking, writing, and talking about their teaching; observing the acts of their own and others' teaching; and by gauging the impact of their teaching on their students' learning.

In these ways, teachers can begin to locate themselves within their profession and start to take more responsibility for shaping their practice. This I call *reflective teaching* (note that I use the terms *reflection, reflective practice, reflective inquiry,* and *reflective teaching* interchangeably).

Reflection Break 2
Feelings About Teaching

- Do you ever feel helpless about your teaching situation and your role as a teacher? If so, why?
- Do you see yourself as a teacher working in an impersonal education system? If so, how do you deal with the system?
- Do you know anyone considering leaving the teaching profession and their reasons for this?
- Do you personally know any teachers who have quit the profession? If so, why did they say they were leaving teaching?
- Do you know how you can take more control of your teaching situation?
- Do you that think reflecting on your teaching (both inside and outside the classroom) can help you take more control of your teaching life? If so, how?
- What advice would you give to new teachers on how to keep themselves fresh throughout their teaching life?

REFLECTIVE TEACHING

Take a few moments to answer the questions posed in Reflection Break 3 before reading on.

Reflection Break 3
Are You a Reflective Teacher?

- Are you a reflective teacher? How do you define the role?
- If you consider yourself to be a reflective teacher, how do you reflect?

- Can you outline any recent examples of your reflections on your teaching?
- Which topics are important for you to reflect upon?
- If you do not consider yourself a reflective teacher at this moment in time, what future plans do you have (if any) to become a more reflective teacher?
- Do you think that reflecting on your teaching is worth doing? Why or why not?
- What benefits do you think you might gain as a result of reflecting on your work?
- What would be the most difficult challenge to reflecting on your work?

Are you a reflective teacher? Reflective teaching requires that teachers examine their values and beliefs about teaching and learning so that they can take more responsibility for their actions in the classroom (Korthagen, 1993). This practice frees teachers from impulsive and routine activity and enables them to act in a more deliberate and intentional manner (Dewey, 1933/1958). Experience itself is actually not the "greatest teacher," for we do not learn as much from experience as we learn from reflecting on that experience.

There is no question that when teachers combine experience with reflection, professional growth is certain (Dewey, 1933/1958), resulting in more effective teaching. Continuing in the spirit of Dewey, Valli (1997) has observed that reflective teachers "can look back on events, make judgments about them, and alter their teaching behaviors in light of craft, research, and ethical knowledge" (p. 70). Teachers who do not bother to reflect on their work can become slaves to routine and powerless to influence their future careers.

It is much easier for teachers to complain about how bad educational systems are (and many teachers believe that this kind of venting is an act of reflective practice—it is not) than to reflect on their own behaviors, both inside and outside of the classroom. Reflective teachers make a point of becoming aware of the factors that affect their practice so they can improve their teaching and, thereby, positively influence the educational systems in which they work.

Why Is Reflective Teaching Worth Doing?

Some teachers may wonder why they should invest time and effort into reflective practice, time they do not have to spare. Even worse, they may view reflective practice as another "job" they have to complete. If teachers do not take time to reflect on their work, they may become prone to burnout. Classrooms are busy places (Jackson, 1968) with many things happening at each moment of each class. Jackson reminds us that an elementary teacher "engages in as many as 1,000 interpersonal interchanges each day" (p. 11). If a lesson is a dynamic event during which many things occur simultaneously, how can teachers hope to be aware of, and be able to control, everything that happens in their classrooms? A teacher's inability to recognize and attend to all classroom issues can, as Good and Brophy (1991) suggest, result in "self-defeating behavior" (p. 1).

Along with the dynamics of each lesson and the demands on time to prepare for classes, institutional constraints further limit teachers' hours in the day to reflect on their work because there is continued pressure to get through the curriculum. This all contributes to a stressful existence for teachers. It is no wonder that some teachers feel isolated and frustrated and entertain thoughts of leaving the profession. They are primed and ready for burnout. Motivated teachers, however, strive to create opportunities to reflect on their work. It all depends on how much time teachers are willing to invest in their own professional development.

If teachers can become more aware of what happens in their classrooms and can monitor accurately both their own behavior and that of their students, they can function more effectively. This can be achieved by engaging in personal reflection as well as reflective conversation with others. As Jay and Johnson (2002) have noted,

Reflection is a process, both individual and collaborative, involving experience and uncertainty. It is comprised of identifying questions and key elements of a matter that has emerged as significant, then taking one's thoughts into dialogue with oneself and with others. (p. 75)

> ### Reflection Break 4
> ### Teacher Burnout
>
> Burnout can occur when teachers feel tired, depressed, ignored, trapped, anxious, or even just bored (Alschuler, 1980).
>
> - Have you ever experienced the feeling of being burned out from teaching? Describe how you felt.
>
>   If yes, can you outline what you think caused the burnout?
>
>   How did you overcome the feeling (assuming you have overcome it)?
>
> - What advice would you give to help beginning teachers avoid burnout?

THE CLASSROOM, STUDENTS, TEACHERS, AND COMMUNITY

Teaching for any period of time raises a number of questions about the teaching activity itself, the location (classroom) and context in which the activity occurs, and the people involved in the activity. The primary players in education are the teacher and the students, with the parents and school administration performing secondary roles. It is the teachers who have chosen their role as a career, and they may or may not have made a conscious decision to pursue this career. Nevertheless, whether novices or veterans, there comes a time in their lives when they wake up and ask themselves why they are doing what they do (at least, I did!). Teachers may have wanted to ask themselves these questions for some time but either did not have the time to devote to honestly thinking about their lives or feared how they might answer.

Reflection Break 5, "Eleven Questions About You as a Teacher," is a good starting point for teachers who want to begin reflecting on their work. The questions challenge teachers to look within and interrogate their initial decision to choose teaching as a career.

Reflection Break 5
Eleven Questions About You as a Teacher

Answer as many of the following questions about the *what* and *why* of teaching as you can:

1. Why did you become a teacher?
2. Did you want to become a teacher?
3. Do you agree or disagree with the following statement: "Those that can, do; those that can't, teach."? Explain your answer.
4. Can you define what the word "teacher" means to you?
5. If a child asked you to explain your job, how would you describe it?
6. What do your family and friends think about you as a teacher? Do they ever say that you "talk like a teacher" or other such things that may identify you as a teacher?

   If yes, what are they, and what does this tell you about yourself as a teacher?
7. What do you think your students think about you as a teacher?
8. Draw your ideal classroom. What does this drawing tell you about yourself as a teacher?
9. Describe your ideal student?
10. What do you want to accomplish in the future as a teacher?
11. What do you want to be known for as a teacher when you retire (your legacy)?

Now consider these questions:

- Which questions were difficult and which were easy for you to answer? Why?
- What did you learn about yourself as a teacher as a result of answering these questions?
- Do you agree that these questions get to the heart of who you are as a teacher?
- Can you think of any other questions to ask yourself?

The questions posed in Reflection Break 5 are easy to ask, but they're certainly not easy to answer, especially at this stage of your reflections. Nevertheless, it is important to at least ask yourself each question as an important first step to discover who you are as a teacher. It may be a good idea for you to write down your responses to these questions now as this exercise can help activate your prior knowledge (schema) about teaching. Even if your answer to many of the questions is, "I don't know," write it down. It's always beneficial to know where you stand before you embark on a reflective journey. You may want to revisit your answers to these questions a few months after reading this book. When you do, see if you would change any of your answers.

How Do I Become a Reflective Practitioner?

There are many suggestions in the literature covering the methods teachers can adopt to become reflective teachers. In this book, the basic framework involves engagement in a cycle of reflective practice (Smyth, 1987) by asking and answering fundamental questions such as

- What do I do as a teacher? (a description of my practice)
- What does this mean to me? (a look at the theories behind my practice)
- How did I come to be this way? (a look at the influences on my practice)
- How might I do this differently? (a look at my future actions)

Again, these questions are easy to ask but difficult to answer. To answer them, teachers must seek knowledge about their practice that requires in-depth and structured reflections. Effective reflective practitioners go a step beyond simply acknowledging successes and failures in the classroom by striving to figure out why some topics or approaches worked and others did not. Teachers dedicated to understanding their practice and growing professionally should

- Reflect on their theories, values, and beliefs about teaching
- Define what learning means to them
- Examine how their students learn and what enhances this learning or inhibits it

- Examine their teaching and their classrooms by monitoring themselves while teaching and interacting with students, colleagues, supervisors, administrators, and parents
- Engage in conversations with other teachers (and supervisors and administrators) about theories, methods, and approaches to teaching and other influences on their practice
- Read what others have said about various aspects of teaching
- Examine the institution in which they teach as well as the educational policies that the institution advocates and upholds
- Examine the community in which they teach

Reflective practitioners celebrate their professional ups and downs, for both propel them toward professional growth. Reflection, as it is outlined and discussed in this book is, as Goodman (1991) says, "much more than taking a few minutes to think about how to keep pupils quiet and on task" (p. 60). Reflection, Goodman has implied, is a dynamic "way of being in the classroom" (p. 60). In other words, engaging in reflective practice is a lifelong endeavor and not a one-off workshop. For teachers to be considered reflective practitioners, they must possess certain qualities that are absent in teachers who follow routine.

Dewey (1933/1958) has suggested that teachers who want to be reflective practitioners must possess three characteristics (or attitudes). They must be

- Open-minded
- Responsible
- Wholehearted

To be open-minded is to be willing to listen to more than one side of an issue and to give attention to alternative views. To be responsible is to carefully consider the consequences our actions, especially as they impact our students personally, intellectually, and socially. To be wholehearted is to be so committed to an idea or project that we can overcome fears and uncertainties in an effort to make meaningful personal and professional change.

Reflection Break 6
Dewey's Three Characteristics of Reflection

Before you embark on your reflective journey, take a look at Dewey's three characteristics:

1. Open-mindedness (willingness to listen to more than one side)
2. Responsibility (careful consideration of the consequences of our actions)
3. Wholeheartedness (commitment to seek every opportunity to learn)

Now consider these questions:

- What levels of these characteristics do you possess as a teacher now (high, medium, or low)?
- Which of these characteristics do you need to develop more as you continue as a teacher?
- Can you think of other desirable characteristics a reflective practitioner should possess?

As you read and interact with this book, I suggest that you continuously revisit Dewey's three reflective dispositions and assess which characteristics you possess during each reflective activity. I hope you can remain *open-minded* as you read each Reflection Break, take *responsibility* for your own professional development, and even encourage your colleagues to embark on their own reflective journeys. I also hope that you *wholeheartedly* begin to take responsibility for your professional development by looking within before you look outside of yourself.

When you finish this section and the chapters of this book, you may also want to reevaluate the degree to which you possess each of these attributes. As you continue to reflect on your work, I predict you will become wholeheartedly more open-minded because you have taken the responsibility to improve your teaching.

CHAPTER THREE

Preparing Teachers for Reflective Practice

We all follow routine in our lives. Incorporating it into each day makes it easier for us to live, but with time, it gets boring. Teachers also follow routine in their teaching lives: It helps that teacher manage the tasks of conducting many classes each day and grading mountains of papers each week. Routine in how classes are conducted also helps the students follow what is going on in class and gives them an idea of what to expect each day. A problem arises, however, when teaching becomes so habitual that it is tantamount to a mechanical act.

Zeichner and Liston (1987) have suggested that "routine action is guided primarily by tradition, external authority and circumstance" but that reflective action "entails the active, persistent and careful consideration of any belief or supposed form of knowledge" (p. 24). Many teachers may not be aware that they are practically on automatic pilot in their classrooms, as they never take time to look closely at their teaching practices. One way of identifying routine, and of counteracting burnout, is by engaging in reflective teaching.

This chapter provides some context, briefly outlining the general education knowledge base of reflective practice over the past twenty years. It addresses its origins, the debate over different definitions and approaches, various models of reflective practice, and criticisms and cautions.

14

> ### Reflection Break 7
> ### How Routine Are You in Your Teaching?
>
> - Have you ever gone into a class to teach without any preparation? If yes, why did you do this and how did the class go?
> - Do you usually (or ever) follow routine ways of teaching?
> - Are you aware of any routines in your teaching?
> - Do you start your classes the same way each day?
> - Do you end your classes the same way each day?
> - Do you go through the textbook page by page? If not, what do you do with the prescribed textbooks you must use?
> - Do you stand or sit in the same place each class?
> - Do you call on the same students to answer questions?
> - Do you tell the same jokes in different classes?
> - Do you keep the same materials year after year and continuously use them in your classes?
> - When was the last time you actively looked for new materials for your classes?
> - Do you think that teachers should follow routine in their teaching and use of materials (textbooks, etc.)? Explain your answer.
> - When was the last time you stopped for a moment and questioned why you were doing what you were doing in the classroom (regarding both methods and materials)?

REFLECTIVE PRACTICE: THE BEGINNING

It is difficult to say exactly where reflective practice for teachers originated, but the work of American educator John Dewey (1933/1958) greatly influenced an increase in its popularity for U.S. teachers. Dewey pointed out that reflection "involves not simply a sequence of ideas but a consequence—a consecutive ordering in such a way that each determines the next as its proper outcome, while each outcome in turn leans back on, or refers to its predecessors" (p. 4).

Argyris and Schon (1974) further developed Dewey's (1933/1958) idea by introducing the notion of *single-loop* and *double-loop learning.* Single-loop learning involves planning and teaching, and evaluating these on a private, almost tacit, level. In double-loop learning, these three aspects of reflection—as well as the discrepancies within and among them—are dealt with on an explicit, publicly accessible level. The tacit is made explicit either by engaging in individual reflective practice or reflecting with others.

Schon (1983) later said that some of the double-loop learning discrepancies (e.g., the lack of connection between a teacher's beliefs and his or her actual classroom practices) caused problems for practitioners in real-world practice. Schon defined a problem as any "puzzling, or troubling, or interesting phenomenon with which the individual is trying to deal" (p. 50). However, Schon came to realize that such discrepancies are not problems in the sense that they can be examined scientifically and that neat and clean solutions can be found for them. Instead, these dilemmas must be solved by improvising, inventing, and testing—entering a reflective cycle, so to speak.

In the United States of the late 1970s and early 1980s, the idea of reflective practice became fashionable through the works of Van Manen (1977), Schon (1983, 1990), and Goodman (1984), to name a few. In the 1990s, educators began to study the content of reflection (Brubacher, Case, & Reagan, 1994; Valli, 1997), how teachers think about their practice (e.g., Richert, 1991), and features of reflection within various teacher education programs (e.g., Ladson-Billings, 1999). Most educators agree that some form of reflection is a desirable practice for teachers. However, the agreement ends there because there is no consensus as to the exact definition of reflection (Hatton & Smith, 1995; Jay & Johnson, 2002).

The focus of reflective practice seems to have dulled somewhat in the late 1990s, with some people in education believing it was just one more bandwagon that administrators and university researchers jumped on. It has become unclear just what reflective practice really means to the practicing teacher. Therefore, it is important for teachers and teacher educators to examine their understanding of the term and perhaps to redefine it in order to make clear their stances on reflective practice. Following Reflection Break 8 is a brief outline of what some educators have said about the reflective practice debate.

Reflection Break 8
Bandwagons and Reflection

- Do you think reflective practice has become another bandwagon issue in education? Why or why not?
- If most educators agree that some form of reflection is desirable, why do you think that there is so much confusion regarding exactly what reflective practice is?

REFLECTIVE PRACTICE: THE DEBATE

Inside or Outside the Classroom?

There are several definitions of reflective practice in the field of education, each carrying a different set of values. Cruickshank and Applegate (1981) characterized reflection as a process that "help[s] teachers to think about what happened, why it happened, and what else could have been done to reach their goals" (p. 553). Gore (1987) found this definition appealing but fundamentally misleading because it did not take societal influence into consideration. Herein lies a major point of contention. Should teachers *only* reflect on specific events within the confines of the classroom, or should they also include the influence of the social and political contexts of the programs as well as the schools and communities in which they teach?

Zeichner and Liston (1996) seemed to side with Gore (1987), acknowledging that Cruickshank and Applegate's (1981) definition emphasized teachers' behavioral skills while excluding the critical issue of linking teaching to the larger community. Smyth (1987) concurred, asserting that emphasizing only the behavioral aspect of teaching was passive and reductive. He advocated an approach toward reflection that is "both active and militant" (p. 3). Rather than taking sides, Bartlett (1990) offered an explanation of what reflection at the individual and societal levels entails. He proposed that "the first relationship involves the subjective meanings in teachers' heads. The second relationship consciously explores the relationship between individual teaching actions and the purposes of education in society" (p. 204).

Reflection Break 9
Reflection Inside and Outside the Classroom

Some educators say that teachers should reflect only on their classroom teaching, whereas other educators say that teachers should also take societal influence into consideration.

- Where do you stand on this issue?

Critical Reflection

Within the reflective practice debate lies the contested notion of *critical reflection* and the ways in which it differs from reflection. Hatton and Smith (1995) put forth their own definition of critical reflection by stating that many educators do "tak[e] it to mean more than constructive self-criticism of one's actions with a view to improvement" (p. 35). They went on to insist that critical reflection "implies the acceptance of a particular ideology" (p. 35). This view also called for consideration of moral and ethical issues (Van Manen, 1977) that puts educators in the position of "making judgments about whether professional activity is equitable, just, and respectful of persons or not" (Hatton & Smith, 1995, p. 35).

More recently, Jay and Johnson (2002) reinforced the notion that critical reflection involves taking in the broader historical, sociopolitical, and moral context of schooling. They suggested that reflective teachers who take this broader view "come to see themselves as agents of change, capable of understanding not only what is, but also working to create what should be" (p. 80). For example, if teachers want to reflect on student performance, they should not only consider the perspectives of the obvious main players (the teacher, the student, and the parents), but they should also consider school culture to include wider socio-historical and politico-cultural contexts in critical reflection (Jay & Johnson, 2002; Schon, 1983, 1990; Zeichner & Liston, 1987, 1996).

Reflection Break 10
Critical Reflection

- What is your understanding of the terms *reflection* and *critical reflection*? Do they mean the same to you?
- What does the word *critical* connote?
- Do you think society can influence what teachers actually do in their classrooms? If not, why not? If so, how?

Reflective Practice: Some Models

Schon

One of the most influential writers on reflection for teachers in recent times, Donald Schon (1983, 1990) drew on the writings of Dewey (1933/1958). Schon (1983, 1990) has written about reflective practice in terms of the immediacy of the action in the setting. He said that teachers, when confronted with nonroutine problems in their classrooms, engage in a process called *problem setting*. Clarke (1995) explained problem setting as going "through a spiraling process of framing and reframing" (p. 245). More recently, other researchers (e.g., Buckley, 1999; Jay & Johnson, 2002;) have agreed with Schon (1983, 1990) that reflection involves framing and reframing.

Reflection Break 11
Schon's Framing and Reframing in Reflection

Schon's (1983, 1990) ideas of framing and reframing are well known. Based on these ideas, Clarke (1995) suggests that "A Teacher Is Reflective When" (p. 246) he or she

1. Is curious or intrigued about some aspect of the practice setting
2. Frames the aspect in terms of the particulars of the setting
3. Reframes that aspect in light of past knowledge or previous experience
4. Develops a plan for future action

(Continued)

(Continued)

Now consider these questions:

- Think of a recent problem in your classroom that intrigued you.
- Frame the problem in terms of the setting that you were in and how the setting may have influenced the onset of the problem.
- Reframe the problem in light of some previous experiences you may have had with similar problems.
- Develop a plan of action that may help you should the problem occur again.

Van Manen

According to Van Manen (1991), reflective practitioners are professionals who reflect in action their constant decision making guided by the theoretical and practical principles of their discipline.

Reflection Break 12
Van Manen's Types of Reflection

Three of Van Manen's (1991) types or levels of reflection are as follows:

Type 1: Anticipatory reflection

Anticipatory reflection allows a teacher to plan, decide a course of action, and anticipate future consequences of the actions.

Type 2: Active or interactive reflection

Active or interactive reflection allows a teacher to make immediate decisions during class as events unfold.

Type 3: Recollective reflection

Recollective reflection allows a teacher to make sense of past experiences and give new, deeper insight into the meaning of those experiences.

Now consider these questions:

- Have you engaged in any of these three types of reflection? If yes, explain.
- If you have never tried any of these types of reflection, can you give an example for each type of reflection that a teacher might engage in?

Zeichner and Liston

Zeichner and Liston (1996) take a different approach, relying on reflective practitioners to uncover their own personal theories and make them explicit. To their credit, Zeichner and Liston acknowledge that this is very difficult to accomplish. Nevertheless, they believe that reflective teachers must seek to find where and how their personal theories originated and subsequently question those theories, especially as they influence practice.

Reflection Break 13
Zeichner and Liston's Dimensions of Reflection

Zeichner and Liston (1996, pp. 44-47) identify a five-level model of different dimensions of reflective practice:

1. **Rapid reaction:** Something happens and a teacher acts instinctively. The teacher's response is immediate in reflection and action.

2. **Repair:** The teacher pauses to think about what happened and may try to repair the situation.

3. **Review:** The teacher takes time out (hours or days) to assess the situation.

4. **Research:** The teacher researches the situation in all its forms, systematically.

5. **Retheorize and research:** The teacher rethinks the situation in light of what he or she has discovered during

(Continued)

(Continued)

the previous four levels of reflection and engages in long-term reflection while looking at what others have done.

Now consider these questions:

- Look at the foregoing five dimensions of reflection. Some educators have said that teachers generally do not proceed beyond the first two levels. Why do you think this may be?
- Have you experienced reflection at any of the five levels?

If yes, describe your experiences.

If no, suggest a possible scenario that may occur at each of these levels (outline a problem that may occur in your teaching).

Jay and Johnson

Jay and Johnson (2002) have talked about a typology that profiles three dimensions of reflective thought: descriptive reflection, comparative reflection, and critical reflection.

Reflection Break 14
Jay and Johnson's Typology of Reflective Practice

Jay and Johnson (2002) have outlined a systematic classification of reflective thought, profiling three dimensions:

1. **Descriptive reflection** involves describing a situation or problem.

2. **Comparative reflection** involves thinking about the situation from different perspectives. Teachers try to solve a problem while also questioning their values and beliefs.

3. **Critical reflection** involves teachers looking at all the different perspectives of a situation or problem and at all of the players involved: teachers, students, the school, and the community.

Now consider these questions:

- Have you found yourself reflecting at these different levels? For what reasons?
- Do you think that it is possible for a teacher to reflect at all three levels? Why or why not?
- Which would be the most difficult level for you within this typology? Explain.
- Have you ever tried to access your own values and beliefs about teaching (not just the problem or situation that caused you to reflect)?
- If yes, how did you accomplish this and what did you discover?

Much of the discussion presented so far assumes a positive correlation between reflective teaching and teacher effectiveness. Now that you have read about some of the models of reflective practice, an important question arises as to how reflective practitioners might be recognized. Part of the answer lies in how they teach and how they talk about teaching. What else might be involved? Reflection Break 15 gives you a chance to answer these questions for yourself.

Reflection Break 15
Recognizing a Reflective Teacher

- How would you define the methods and approaches of a reflective practitioner? Explain.
- Although there is a certain amount of overlap in the four models for reflection presented in this chapter, which of them appeals to you most? Why?
- Have you put any of these models into practice? If yes, please explain your level of engagement and the outcome.
- Can you suggest any alternative models of reflective practice?

Reflective Practice: Some Criticisms and Cautions

A number of scholars have urged caution as to the applicability of reflective practice in education. For example, Jackson (1968) challenged the notion that more reflective teachers are better teachers. Jackson argues that "If they did posses the inclinations and skills for reflection . . . they might receive greater applause from intellectuals, but it is doubtful that they would perform with greater efficiency in the classroom" (p. 151). However, Zeichner (1981) attacked Jackson's stance of giving primacy to efficiency in evaluating the worth of reflective teaching, stating that it does not take into account the value of reflection in making teachers more thoughtful about their practice.

Nevertheless, some educators have remained skeptical of the benefits of reflection (e.g., Doyle & Ponder, 1977). Although Van Manen (1991) said that it is possible for teachers to be both active and reflective during a class, Doyle and Ponder (1977) suggested that most teachers would not be aware of this level of reflection because it occurs unconsciously during class. They explained that reflection of the type Van Manen (1991) wrote about—interactive reflection—may not be practicable because reflection and action cannot occur simultaneously. A teacher who reflects too often and for significant periods of time in the classroom may be creating a dysfunctional classroom. Hoover (1994) also critiqued reflective practice for educators, claiming that "The promising acclamation about reflection has yielded little research qualitatively or quantitatively" (p. 83). However, since his commentary in 1994, many education journals have shown increased attention to research on teacher reflection and reflective practice (e.g., Farrell, 1999; Jay & Johnson, 2002; Ladson-Billings, 1999; Valli, 1999).

Reflection Break 16
Reflective Practice—Some Criticisms and Cautions

Hatton and Smith (1995) list three "barriers which hinder the achievement of reflective approaches" (p. 36), stated as follows:

1. Reflection is a more academic exercise and, as such, is seen as "research." They argue that teachers do not see the need for conducting such research.

2. Teachers need time and opportunity for development. At the moment they do not have this extra time available in most fast-paced school settings.

3. Discussions of successes and failures with a group of strangers (such as reflecting with other teachers) can lead to vulnerability.

Now consider these questions:

- Which of the arguments outlined above do you agree with and why?
- Which of the arguments do you disagree with and why?
- Can you think of any other criticisms and cautions that teachers should think about with regard to reflective practice? List them.

CHAPTER FOUR

Getting Started With Reflective Practice

As you now know, teachers have been practicing reflection for quite some time. This does not mean, however, that all educators are in agreement as to what exactly is involved in reflecting. Even though there is some overlap in what educators say reflection entails, there is no unity when it comes to agreeing on a definition of reflective practice. This is not necessarily a bad thing, for it allows teachers to define for themselves what reflection means. Educators Jay and Johnson (2002) have argued that educators must accept, in general, that "the concept [of reflection] is not clearly defined," but if each person tries to "clarify [his or her own] understanding of reflection" (p. 73), it can be made personally meaningful. It is necessary that *each* teacher who engages in reflection attempts to define the concept from his or her unique point of view. In this chapter, I strive to define what the concept of reflective practice means to me by first outlining some common ideas evident in most of the existing definitions and then outlining my own definitions.

Reflection Break 17
Understanding Reflective Practice

- What is your understanding of reflective practice?
- What does reflection mean to you as a teacher?
- What is your definition of reflection?

Compare your answers with what you read next in the text.

UNDERSTANDING REFLECTIVE PRACTICE

Zeichner and Liston (1996) emphasized the reason for engaging in reflective practice:

> For in order to understand and direct our educational practices, we need to understand our own beliefs and understandings. So much of teaching is rooted in who we are and he how we perceive the world. (p. 23)

How can we access our own beliefs and then put those beliefs into practice in the classroom? One way is to look at reflection as systematic and structured. We cannot hope to bring our beliefs and values about teaching from a tacit level without systematically looking at our teaching. Taggart and Wilson (1998) suggested that definitions of reflective practice should also have change or self-improvement as a final goal. Putting these concepts together in one definition, reflective practice is a systematic and structured process in which we look at concrete aspects of teaching and learning with the overall goal of personal change and more effective practice. By change, I do not only mean behavioral adaptations toward teaching methods. Hopefully, we change as a result of the *awareness* brought about by engaging in reflection.

For the purposes of this book, reflective practice seeks answers to the following questions:

- What am I doing in the classroom (method)?
- Why am I doing this (reason)?
- What is the result?
- Will I change anything based on the information gathered from answering the first three questions (justification)?

These questions for self-analysis can be schematically represented as follows:

1. Method ⇒ Reason ⇒ Result ⇒ Justification

This approach to reflective practice begins with what the teacher actually does in a classroom (method). Understanding the reasons, results, and justification for these actions involves reflecting on "the wider issues in education—its aims, its social and personal consequences, its ethics, the rationale of its methods and its curricula—and the intimate relationship between these and the immediate reality" of a teacher's classroom practice (Parker 1997, pp. 30-31).

Reflection Break 18
Reflection and Action

- What one word is common to all four types of reflective practice outlined in Table 4.1?
- What does that word tell you about reflective practice?
- Reiman (1999) has proposed that there should be a balance between action and reflection. How do you think you can manage to balance action and reflection inside and outside the classroom?

Types of Reflective Practice

There are four major approaches to the study of reflective practice (Table 4.1 summarizes and compares them).

Table 4.1   Summary of Different Approaches to Reflective Teaching

Reflection Type	Content of Reflection
Reflection-in-action Schon (1983, 1990)	Making decisions about events in the classroom as they happen
Reflection-on-action Hatton and Smith (1995) (Schon 1983, 1990)	Thinking about one's teaching after the class; giving reasons for one's actions and behaviors in class
Reflection-for-action Killon and Todnew (1991)	Proactive thinking in order to guide future action
Action research Dana and Yendol-Silva (2003) McFee (1993) Sagor (1993) Cochran-Smith and Lytle (1993) Carr and Kemmis (1986)	Investigating in detail one topic related to one's classroom teaching

The first type of reflective practice is called *reflection-in-action* (Schon 1983, 1990). This practice requires that the teacher employ a kind of knowing-in-action (Schon, 1983, 1990). According to Schon, knowing-in-action occurs when we recognize a face in a crowd without "listing" and piecing together separate features. We don't think, "Could that be. . . ?"—we just know. However, if you were asked to describe the features that prompted this recognition, it might be difficult because, as Schon has pointed out, that type of information usually remains at the tacit level.

Reflection Break 19
Listing Features to Aid Reflection-in-Action

This Reflection Break (adapted from Schon, 1983, 1990) highlights the difficulties that may be encountered trying to describe the things seen each day and usually take for granted.

- Try to list the features of your best friend's face.
- Was it easy? Why or why not?

Again according to Schon (1983, 1990), there is a sequence of "moments" in a process of reflection-in-action:

- A situation or action occurs which triggers spontaneous, routine responses (such as in knowing-in-action):

  A student cannot answer a question about a topic he or she has explained in great detail during the previous class.

- Routine responses (i.e., what the teacher has always done) produce a surprise:

  The teacher starts to explain how the student had already explained this topic the previous class and that this silence was troubling. The student now begins to cry. This gets the teacher's attention.

- This surprise leads to reflection within an action:

  The teacher reacts quickly to try to find out why the student is suddenly crying by questioning the student or asking the student's classmates why they think the student is crying.

- Reflection gives rise to on-the-spot experimentation:
    The student may or may not explain why he or she is crying. The teacher will take some measures (depending on the reaction or nonreaction) to help solve the problem: ignore the situation, empathize with the student, help the student answer the question by modeling answers, and so forth.

Reflection Break 20
Reflecting on Moments That Happen During Class

- Have you ever been teaching a class when something happened that you were not expecting? If so, explain the event to another teacher or write an account of what happened (or both).
- How did you respond?
- What was the result of your response?

The second type of reflection is called *reflection-on-action* and involves thinking back on what was done to discover how knowing-in-action may have contributed to an unexpected action (Hatton & Smith, 1995; Schon, 1990). Here, teachers reflect on their classes after they have finished.

Reflection Break 21
Reflecting on Moments That Happen After Class

- What kind of reflecting do you do (if any) immediately after teaching a class?
- Do you ever talk to other teachers after class about teaching? What do you talk about?
- Do you ever talk to students about their perceptions of your class and teaching? What do you talk about?

- Do you ever ask students to tell you what they think they learned in your class?
- Do you ever write about your teaching in a diary?
- Have you ever gathered data on your class and discussed your findings with another colleague? If so, explain.

The third type of reflection is called *reflection-for-action*. Reflection-for-action is different from the previous types of reflection in that it is proactive in nature. Killon and Todnew (1991) argue that reflection-for-action is the desired outcome of both previous types of reflection; they say that "we undertake reflection, not so much to revisit the past or to become aware of the meta cognitive process one is experiencing (both noble reasons in themselves) but to guide future action (the more practical purpose)" (p. 15). Teachers can prepare for the future by using knowledge from what happened during class and what they reflected on after class. As such, reflective teaching is useful for detecting inconsistencies between belief and practice.

The fourth type of reflection is *action research*. Action research and reflective teaching practice are closely connected. Action research is the investigation of those craft knowledge values of teaching (what is actually done in the classroom) that hold teaching habits in place (McFee, 1993). It requires the transformation of research into action. Action research is one answer to the problematic reality that teachers' voices are absent from the research literature on teaching (Zeichner & Liston, 1996). Teachers should be seen as thinking professionals who can "both pose and solve problems related to their educational practice" (Zeichner & Liston, 1996, p. 4). Teachers can pose such problems related to their practice by entering into a reflective exploration cycle.

The general stages of the reflective cycle of the action research process are as follows:

- **Identify** (identify the problem)
- **Plan** (decide on the method you are going to use to investigate the problem you identified)
- **Research** (review the literature, consult colleagues)
- **Observe** (collect data—classroom observations, journal writing, discussions)

- **Reflect** (analyze the data)
- **Act** (redefine the problem and take some action)
- **Repeat** (go through the cycle again to see what the new actions have yielded)

When the teacher recognizes a need to investigate a problem, he starts to plan how to investigate ways of solving this problem. The teacher begins by reading background literature on the problem to formulate ideas on how to solve it. This research cycle should include talking to colleagues about the concern, as they may have advice to offer. The teacher then plans a strategy to collect data. Once the data have been collected, the teacher analyzes and reflects on them, making a data-driven decision to take action; this step in the cycle involves redefining the problem.

After going through this process, teachers will take more responsibility for the decisions they make in their classes because they are informed decisions, not based on feeling or impulse.

Reflection Break 22
Action Research for the Busy Teacher

- Try to think of a few action research projects you might like to attempt. Make a list.

For example:

1. **Investigate** the types of questions you ask.
2. **Note and analyze** the amount of time you wait ("wait-time") for student responses after asking a question.
3. **Test** which kinds of groups work best in your classroom (e.g., grouping by gender, by age, by size, etc.).

Now consider the following:

- Choose a problem or a focus for your action research project and examine the action research reflective cycle summarized below. See if you can complete one cycle of action research:

1. Identify a problem (or focus).
2. Collect data (information) systematically about the problem.
3. Examine, analyze and interpret the information gathered in order to reflect on what the information tells you.
4. Act on the information by making some changes to improve your teaching.

- Reflect on the changes by going though one more cycle.

Levels of Reflection

Once teachers have chosen a particular type of reflection, the next question presents itself: How deeply should they reflect? Reflective practice here is split into three hierarchical levels, as outlined in Figure 4.1: action, conceptual, and ethical. These three levels are similar to Jay and Johnson's (2002) typology of reflection, which profiles three dimensions of reflective thought: descriptive reflection, comparative reflection, and critical reflection.

Figure 4.1 shows that the basic level of reflection, Level 1, is action in the classroom. When teachers plan at the level of action, they are concerned only with what they do in the classroom. When teachers reflect at Level 1, often called *technical rationality*, they focus on their behavior and skills within the classroom. Level 2, the conceptual level, involves analyzing the reasons for the actions taken. When teachers reflect at Level 2, often called *reflection at a contextual level*, they focus on the theory behind their classroom practices. Teachers can then look into alternative practices they might prefer to use, depending on their students' needs. Level 3 encourages teachers to justify the work they do and reflect within the broader context of society. When teachers reflect at Level 3, often called *critical* or *dialectical reflection*, they focus on the moral, ethical, and sociopolitical issues associated with their practice, looking at outside forces in order to gain greater self-understanding.

It may be possible for teachers to reflect on different levels simultaneously, depending on the topic of reflection (hence the multidirectional arrows). New teachers may find themselves reflecting at the Level 1, the level of action, as they may not have enough time

Figure 4.1   Hierarchical Levels of Reflection

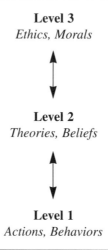

Level 3
Ethics, Morals

Level 2
Theories, Beliefs

Level 1
Actions, Behaviors

SOURCE: Adapted from Day, 1993

or space to reflect at the conceptual level (Level 2) or moral level (Level 3). This is a normal level of reflection for new teachers, as they are just developing their schemata of teaching. In time, they will find themselves reflecting at each of the various levels.

Reflection Break 23
Levels of Reflection

- Now is a good time for you to explore your level of reflective thinking. The hierarchical levels of reflection are as follows (see Taggart & Wilson, 1998, for a detailed questionnaire regarding the different levels of reflection):

Level 1: The level of a teacher's actions in the classroom—a teacher's observable behaviors

Level 2: The theoretical level—the theories behind the teacher's behaviors in Level 1

Level 3: The ethical, moral level—the role of the wider community in influencing a teacher's theories (Level 1) and practices (Level 2)

Now consider these questions:

- Give an example of how a teacher could operate at each of the three levels.
- Which level of reflection do you find yourself working at now?
- What does this mean to you as a reflective teacher?
- Do you think a teacher should always operate (reflect) at any particular level? Explain.

In this chapter, I have discussed definitions of reflection, shown how it is systematic, and gauged the levels of reflective practice for teachers. I have also suggested why reflective practice has value. However, teachers must define (or even redefine) what reflective practice means to them and how they can best practice reflection in order to improve their teaching.

Reflection Break 24
What Does Reflection Mean to You?

Now that you have read some of the literature on reflection and reflective practice, write what reflection means to you as a teacher and how you would engage in reflective practice.

CHAPTER FIVE

Providing Opportunities for Reflective Practice

If, as the previous chapters have suggested, reflective practice is seen as a means for teachers to examine their beliefs, values, and teaching practices, then they must be presented with opportunities that enable them carry out those reflections systematically. There are many suggestions in the literature as to how teachers can go about reflecting on their practice, some more systematic than others. But not one provides an overall framework for teachers to use when reflecting on their work—whether individually, in pairs, or in teams. This chapter outlines a model of reflective practice, with five core components, that teachers can use to reflect on practice.

Reflection Break 25
Opportunities to Reflect

- Think of several reflective methods and activities that teachers might use. List them.
- Have you ever used any of these methods or activities? If yes, explain how.
- Which of these methods would be easy and quick for you to use?
- Which of the methods would be more complicated for you to use (and thus take longer)?

Examples: journal writing, self-observation, classroom observations, pair or group discussions.

THE FARRELL MODEL OF REFLECTIVE PRACTICE

The five components of this model of reflective practice (Farrell, 1999) are as follows:

1. Providing different opportunities for teachers to reflect through a range of different activities

2. Building ground rules into the process and into each activity

3. Making provisions for four different categories of time

4. Providing external input for enriched reflection

5. Providing for low affective states

Note in the representation of the model in Figure 5.1 that the five core elements are interconnected—one builds on the other, and all should be considered as a whole.

Figure 5.1   Model of Reflective Practice for Teachers

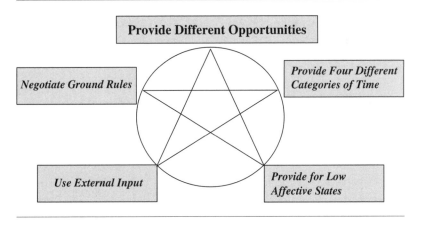

It is important to mention that teachers reflecting alone, in pairs, or as members of teams or groups can all adapt this model to suit their own needs. As the different components of the model are outlined and discussed, teachers can decide where their reflective needs and styles fit into each component. For example, if a teacher wants to reflect alone, then there is no need to follow the suggestions for pairs (critical friends) or groups.

Reflection Break 26
The Farrell Model of Reflective Practice

Look at the five components of the model of reflective practice that follow. What is your understanding of each component?

1. Providing different opportunities for teachers to reflect, through a range of different activities
2. Building ground rules into the process and into each activity
3. Making provisions for four different categories of time
4. Providing external input for enriched reflection
5. Providing for low affective states

Now consider these questions:

- What is your opinion of the model as a whole?
- Outline an argument that explains why each component is or isn't necessary.
- Add more components to this model. Outline your own model of reflective practice.

Providing Different Opportunities for Teachers to Reflect Through a Range of Different Activities

The first, and main, component of the model suggests that teachers can engage in a range of activities that facilitate reflection. These activities include group discussions (Chapter 6), classroom observations (Chapter 7), journal writing (Chapter 8), and creating teaching portfolios (Chapter 9). However, teachers who may want to reflect alone can omit the sections on group discussions, and then return to them later when deciding whether or not to share individual findings and get feedback from groups.

- **Group discussions**, in which teachers talk to other teachers, are by definition collaborative and orally based and are highly beneficial for teachers interested in practicing reflection.

During oral inquiry, teachers build on one another's insights to analyze and interpret classroom data (from audio or video recordings) and their experiences in the school. The main benefit of forming pairs or teams is that discussion and collaboration within a pair or a group of peers can facilitate the sharing of different knowledge, skills, expertise and viewpoints, especially if these viewpoints do not always coincide. When viewpoints differ, pairs or group members can have the experience of looking at the same topic or problem from angles that they would not have had reflecting alone.

- **Classroom observations** means just that: teachers looking at what goes on in classrooms, reviewing concrete data related to classes. Individual teachers, pairs, or groups can engage in classroom observations, but individual teachers can only watch videotapes of their own classes. The data should consist of descriptions of classroom events, thereby avoiding judgments about what should or should not occur in a class. These descriptions of teaching can be analyzed and interpreted by the teacher (if reflecting alone) or by pairs and teams working together. Descriptions may be verbal or written, depending on the purpose of the observation. If the purpose of the observation is to become more informed teachers, then strictly critical judgments should be suspended. Many teachers have come to fear the evaluative aspect of classroom observation, preventing them from using observation as a method of self-improvement. Teachers are encouraged to videotape or audiotape their classes or both. Later, they can describe, analyze, and interpret the information they have recorded. Pairs of teachers can also team up in critical friendships (covered in depth in Chapter 7) to discuss teaching. These critical friends can challenge each other in positive ways, in a safe environment, so that both friends grow as teachers. The main emphasis here is on the friend aspect rather than the critical.

- **Teaching journals** are excellent tools to aid reflection. They are simple to create and maintain and can promote the development of reflective teaching. Individuals, pairs, and groups can use teaching journals when reflecting on their work. Teachers can write in their journals at any time of the working day or after. They can record criticisms, doubts, frustrations, questions, the joys of teaching, and the results of experiments.

- **Teaching portfolios** are excellent for putting together a collection of evidence of development in teaching expertise in one document. They can contain an unlimited variety of materials, including lists of courses taught, teaching innovations, personal teaching philosophies, evidence of successes, and evidence of commitment to professional development. Teaching portfolios foster reflection because to compile them, teachers must examine their professional strengths and weaknesses; thus they become more aware of their work.

Reflection Break 27
Reflection Activities

The Farrell Model of Reflective Practice suggests that individual teachers, pairs of teachers, and teams of teachers can engage in the following activities as opportunities for reflection:

1. Group discussions

2. Journal writing

3. Classroom observations (critical friendships)

4. Teaching portfolios

Now consider these questions:

- What do you think a teacher (or a pair or group of teachers) would have to do in each activity?
- In your view, which activity would be easiest and which would be hardest for teachers to use to reflect on their work?
- Can you list some other activities that teachers could try when reflecting on their work.

As noted, providing opportunities for teachers to reflect is the main component of the Farrell Model of Reflective Practice. However, the four remaining components play critical roles in establishing an atmosphere that encourages the effective implementation and practice of reflective activities. These components, as seen in Figure 5.1, instruct teachers to

- Negotiate ground rules
- Provide for four different categories of time
- Use external input
- Provide for low affective states

Negotiating Ground Rules

There is a need for a negotiated set of built-in rules or guidelines that each group should follow in order to benefit all members. Different rules must be established for group meetings, classroom observation, depth of journal writing, and critical friendships.

Reflection Break 28
Ground Rules for Reflective Activities

It's important to set guidelines if reflective practice is to be consistent and clear. Let's say you're deciding between writing in a journal once a day or once a week, or maybe you've committed to helping observe another teacher's classroom. By determining some ground rules, you can ensure efficient and effective practice.

- What would be required in each of the reflective activities (group discussions, journal writing, classroom observations, and critical friendships) from an individual teacher? A pair of teachers? A group of teachers?

Now compare your list of ground rules with what is presented in the following pages.

Group Discussions

Who will chair the meetings? Some groups might select a different chairperson for each meeting who is responsible for providing a meeting location, bringing refreshments, and setting the agenda and length of the meeting. The chairperson can also use the position to protect and encourage the free expression of opinion.

Classroom Observation

Certain understandings need to be negotiated ahead of time. For example, what are the responsibilities of the observer? Is intervention possible or desirable in the class? Will the class be videotaped, audiotaped, or neither? If you use a video camera, how will the tape be analyzed and why? What is to be observed and how?

Journal Writing

A minimum set of guidelines needs to be negotiated to guarantee a level of reflection beyond mere descriptions of teaching (Level 1; see Chapter 4). Groups should decide on the frequency and types of entries. To reflect beyond description alone, teachers can answer why they teach the way they do (Level 2) and how society, school, and community (Level 3) influence their teaching. A lone teacher writing a journal may have difficulty moving through the different levels and should seek out a critical friend or a group of teachers to deepen the reflection.

Critical Friendship

A set of built-in rules for critical friends is not easily suggested because there must be elements of trust and openness so that the critical aspect does not negatively affect the friendship. Critical friends both support and challenge each other to have more profound reflections on their teaching.

It is difficult to accomplish the described activities and built-in guidelines quickly. This introduces the next component of the model: time.

Provide for Four
Different Categories of Time

For practicing teachers to be able to reflect on their work in groups, time is a very important consideration.

> ## Reflection Break 29
> ## Time Factors That Affect Reflection
>
> - What time factors do you think would be important to consider when starting a teacher development group to reflect on practice?
> - Consider the time factors for each of the reflection activities presented in the previous sections.
> - Compare your answers with what is presented in the following pages.

In the reflective process, time can be broken down into four different categories that help teachers begin thinking about reflective practice and how they intend to maintain it. The four categories are

1. Individual

2. Activity

3. Development

4. Reflection

Individual

Practicing teachers are busy daily with teaching and other related duties. The amount of time any one teacher is willing to invest in his or her professional self-development will naturally vary. Individual teachers can decide for themselves, but this issue becomes very important when teachers form groups to reflect on their work. Such a group may not cohere if all of the participants are not able to attend each meeting or participate fully in the activities. When teachers consider forming groups, they must individually assess the amount of time they will be able to commit to it.

Activity

Associated with the time each participant has to give the project is the time that will be spent on each activity. Again, individual teachers can decide what suits them in time terms for each activity. For pairs and groups of teachers, time for the observation processes will depend on the number of observations they choose to perform. Each group must negotiate the number of times a class can be observed, taking into consideration the amount of individual time each teacher has to give. Journal writing also requires time for individual teachers as well as in pairs and groups. Pairs and groups may decide to set aside a period of time at the beginning or end of meetings for writing and reading journal entries.

Development

Another important consideration is the time it takes to develop these new skills. Golby and Appleby (1995) pointed out that "teachers do not readily confront their problems with a reflective approach" (p. 158). Elbaz (1988) added that teachers "have a common concern to reduce the complexity of the situation, to accept neat and obvious accounts of the causes of the problems" (p. 173). Analytical reflection, therefore, takes time to develop and progresses at a rate specific to each teacher. This may also impact a pair or group of teachers, as individuals within the pair or group may develop at different speeds.

Reflection

When teachers participate in groups to become more reflective practitioners, their reflective time has two aspects. The first involves how often and for how long a period they want to meet as group dedicated to reflective practice. Individual teachers can easily decide for themselves, but groups must unanimously agree. The second aspect of time impacts pairs and groups of teachers: How much time within the group will be devoted to reflection itself? Groups must consider both of these aspects to serve their members best. Both individuals and pairs or groups should realize that it takes time to become adept at reflection and so it is advisable to continue reflecting for at least one semester. This means that groups should meet for several months. In addition, it is a good idea to institute fixed periods of time for reflection during meetings to provide participants with some consistent minimum practice time during the semester.

Reflection Break 30
Period for Reflection

The period for reflection as presented in the previous section depends on four categories of time:

1. Individual—each teacher's invested time in reflection

2. Activity—time spent on each activity

3. Development—time it takes for individual teachers to develop as a result of reflecting on their work

4. Reflection—the block of time given to the reflection exercises available to the individual, pairs, or teams

Now consider the following:

- Which of the four categories of time do you think would be most problematic for you when considering reflecting on your work? Why?
- Think of other time issues that need to be considered when teachers want to reflect on their work. List them.
- How would you go about convincing the administration at your institution that it should provide or allow a sufficient period of time for you and your colleagues to reflect? (Issues raised in Chapters 2 & 3 in this book may give you some pertinent ideas.)

Use External Input

The three preceding components of the model of reflective practice (providing different opportunities, negotiating ground rules, and the four categories of time) encourage teachers to probe and articulate personal theories of teaching, which are at the center of teacher professional self-development. These components constitute a process of constructing and reconstructing real teaching experiences and reflecting on personal beliefs about teaching. While it is important to focus on the personal, teacher reflection also requires input from outside sources: other people's observations and reflections, others' theories, and lessons learned from research and literature on teaching practices.

If groups of teachers readily accept and support each other's opinions regarding their teaching, change may be inhibited. To attain deeper levels of reflection, individuals and groups on the road to professional self-development need to be challenged by input outside of the group. This external input can come from professional journals, other teachers' observations, and published case studies.

Reflection Break 31
External Input to Aid Reflection

Some educators suggest that teachers should not just reflect alone (navel gazing) or in groups (group navel gazing) but that they should also look outside their classes and pairs or groups to learn what others are doing. This means seeking external input.

- What types of external input would be necessary and appropriate for individual and group discussions?
- Where could teachers get this external input?
- What research could you read up on?
- What books and journal articles would be appropriate for you and your group to read?

Have each person in the group draw up a list and then compare them. (See the reference list for suggestions.)

Provide for Low Affective States

Changing teaching practice is not easy. The process takes a long time and is often painful. Inevitably, a certain level of anxiety will be present. In fact, for in-depth reflection to occur, which is not automatic, anxiety may always be present. Therefore, groups should encourage a nonthreatening environment of sharing and collaboration. Ways of establishing low anxiety can be incorporated into meeting decorum, such as consciously emphasizing description and observation over critical judgment. Category systems such as Acheson's and Gall's (1992) SCORE (Seating Chart Observation Record) could also be used to reduce anxiety associated with judgments during group meetings.

Reflection Break 32
Using SCORE With Reflection

To keep anxiety levels low during discussions on classes that were observed, the text suggested the use of a category instrument known as SCORE (Acheson & Gall, 1992).

- First, record your class (using audio or video or both). Then answer the following questions, individually or in pairs or groups, using the SCORE analysis technique described immediately following.

  How many whole-class questions does the teacher ask?

  How many students answer these whole-class questions?

  How many questions directed at individuals does the teacher ask?

  How many students answer these individual questions?

- SCORE Analysis:

  Draw where each student is sitting and where the teacher is in the classroom.

  Every time the teacher asks or answers a question, draw a line from the teacher to the student answering or asking that question.

  Draw lines from student to student if they ask each other questions.

  Count the frequency of the type of each question.

  How many questions are directed at the entire class? At individual students?

  You should be able to see a map of the classroom interaction in terms of questions and answers.

  To which students does the teacher ask the most questions?

  In what area of the classroom do they sit?

CHAPTER SIX

Group Discussion to Aid Reflective Practice

C hapter 5 outlined a model of reflective practice that individuals, pairs, and groups of teachers can follow when exploring various aspects of their work. This model includes the option to reflect alone without the input of others, for it may well be that individuals reflecting on their work for the first time may feel threatened if they have to share their findings. They may feel more comfortable exploring their teaching alone by recording and reflecting on their classes (using audio or video or both) or by keeping a personal journal to reflect on who they are as teachers.

Reflection Break 33
Reflection: Individual or Group?

- Which do you think would be the most effective grouping of teachers for reflective practice: individuals, pairs, or teams or groups of three members or more?
- Outline the advantages and disadvantages of each grouping for reflection.

Here are a few examples, to get you started:

Individual reflections:

Advantages—Safe, focused, on own time. Disadvantages— Nobody to challenge beliefs, too narrow.

Group reflections:

Advantages—Support available from others, sociable. Disadvantages—Possibility of dominating members and agendas, trust issues.

- If you think a group is more effective for teachers to reflect, how many members do you think would be best?

GROUP REFLECTIONS

When teachers have become comfortable looking at their own teaching and have examined their beliefs about teaching, they may feel the need to pair up with another teacher or join a group of teachers to share their reflective experiences. Speier (1973) stated that people "seek each other out for the predominant purpose of talking" (p. 36). Teachers may find it more beneficial to come together in groups or teams to discuss their teaching, especially if the discussion occurs in a supportive atmosphere. However, when a group forms to reflect on work, each member must deal with the issue of trust. Each member must agree to keep in confidence what is disclosed in group meetings. Each group must address and negotiate this ethical issue before embarking on reflections.

Reflection Break 34
Group Reflection With Trust

- Do you think all group members should sign a statement agreeing that none of the results of the group's reflective activities can be disclosed without written permission from each member?

Group Issues

Teaching, by its very nature, can be a lonely affair. Close your eyes and picture yourself at the front of your classroom. More than thirty students could be facing you, but mentally they might be miles away. You're teaching, you're disciplining, and you're making hundreds of decisions each day to students that often seem indifferent, if not hostile. It remains the teacher's sole responsibility to answer for these decisions because contact with colleagues is the exception rather than the rule.

Of course, teachers may wish to reflect individually on their practices, but as Jay and Johnson (2002) remind us, teachers must carefully consider the possible outcomes of reflecting alone versus reflecting with others (collaborative reflection). Although reflecting alone clearly has its advantages, its practitioners are of course more prone to bias (in their own favor) when attempting to reconstruct their practice (Webb, 1999). Cochran-Smith and Lytle (1993) suggest that oral inquiry, such as group discussions, is one method for teachers to reflect on their work:

> Oral inquiry processes are procedures in which two or more teachers jointly research their experiences by examining particular issues, educational concepts, texts (including students' work), and other data about students. . . . They are by definition collaborative and oral. During oral inquiry, teachers build on one another's insights to analyze and interpret classroom data and their experiences in the school as a workplace. (p. 30)

Discussion within a group of peers can be a powerful way of exposing teachers to different viewpoints. When the group members are supportive, these varying points of view are wonderful input. As James (1996) points out, "The person, using the group as solidarity to support others and to be supported, then becomes empowered to act productively elsewhere" (p. 94). Discussions can center on teaching practices as well as the theories and beliefs that are behind those practices.

Reflection Break 35
Group Talking

- Have you ever participated in discussions with other teachers on a regular basis?
  If so, please describe your experiences:

  What did you talk about?

  What was the interaction like?

  What did you gain from the discussions?

  What do you think could have been done better in the group?

- If you have not had any experience in a group, think about what you would hope to accomplish from discussions with other teachers. Answer the previous questions from your perspective:

  What would you like to talk about?

  What type of interaction do you think should be encouraged?

  What do you think you could gain from the discussions?

Group discussions take place when several teachers regularly come together to reflect on their work. A teacher trainer or moderator could provide encouragement and support for the group, but this is not always necessary. When setting up group discussions, it is important to effectively address the issues of leadership and interaction. As Birchak et al. (1998) suggest, successful group facilitators must "develop strategies and language to support others in sharing their experience" (p. 54).

Reflection Break 36
Setting Up a Group

- How will you set up your group? Will you set a minimum and maximum number of members?
- Who will be the leader? Does your group need a leader?

(*Continued*)

(Continued)

- Where will the meetings take place and how often will they be held?
- How will you allow for interaction (turn taking) within the group? Will it be "speak when you want" or will there be strict adherence to turns?

Reflection Break 36 poses questions about setting up a group; they may give the impression that it would be easy to set up such a group. In fact, the opposite is more likely to be true. It is not easy to get a group of teachers together to talk about teaching, and if you do get a group together, it may not be easy to maintain because of the different relationships that may exist within the group. Nieto et al. (2002) liken the relationships within a teacher development group to marriage, family, and a classroom community because "it takes time, patience, tolerance, love, and no small measure of commitment to the process. It means being willing to be exposed, to become frustrated, to disagree, to marvel, and to learn" (p. 344).

Even after teachers have selected the procedures they will follow in setting up a group, touchy issues will arise. These issues need to be dealt with, and participants need to be aware of some of the shortfalls that may occur within the group. Two crucial issues are *group function* and *group interaction*.

Group Function

The group is set up to provide support to all its members as they reflect on their teaching. As such, each group should clearly outline its purpose and objectives. Bring Reflection Break 37 to one of your group meetings, and try answering the questions together.

Reflection Break 37
Purpose of the Group

Why form a group?
- What is the purpose of your group?
- What are some objectives that teachers who come together to talk about their teaching might have?

> Which of these objectives would be the easiest to pursue?
>
> Which would be the most time-consuming?
>
> Which would most likely be successful, given the realities of a teacher's busy schedule?

If a group decides that its purpose is to explore each teacher's practice, that's a good start, but it is too general. Some more specific focuses might include

- The desire to examine and analyze classroom research
- The desire to discuss theories of teaching and learning
- The opportunity to work in a collaborative mode on a research project about classroom teaching

---

Reflection Break 38
Scheduling Group Meetings

- When will the group meet?
- Where will the meetings take place?
- How long will the meetings be?
- Will the group stick strictly to the time decided? If not, what procedures will be put in place to deal with meetings that go overtime?

Group Interaction

An effective group operates for the benefit of all its members and not for any one individual in particular. Group members bring different expectations, fears, and hopes, and not all of these may be transparent to the other members. Accordingly, group members should be sensitive to each other. In addition to differences in expectation, there will be both men and women and a wide range of interests, teaching experiences, abilities, ages, and social backgrounds in each group. The group must respect its diversity.

If groups of teachers come together to discuss and reflect on their teaching, then it is important for them to recognize the various types of interactions that may or may not provide opportunities for reflection. As Senge (1990) says,

> The discipline of dialogue also involves learning how to recognize the patterns of interaction in teams that undermine learning. The patterns of defensiveness are often deeply engrained in how the team operates. If unrecognized, they undermine learning. If recognized and surfaced creatively, they can actually accelerate learning. (p. 10)

Reflection Break 39
Communicating in a Group

One method of assessing the interpersonal climate of the group is by seeking answers to the following questions:

- Who communicated the most in the group?
- Who did not speak very often?
- Who was absent?
- Who asked the most questions?
- Which pairs or groups of three (depending on the number of participants in the group) communicated most?
- How can the group explain these interaction patterns?
- How can the group function even more effectively next time?

The group members must establish ground rules early on that will ensure respect and trust in all discussions, even when controversial issues arise. One way of ensuring that trust is to guarantee that confidentiality will be of utmost importance. Confidentiality means that the group's discussions and writing will be kept within the group and will only be made public if each member of the group gives permission.

Reflection Break 40
Starting and Ending Group Meetings

After researching their own teacher group in action, Oprandy, Golden, and Shiomi (1999) established a set of procedures for collaborative conversations:

- The group leader makes the initial move in the form of an open-ended question, such as "What struck anyone today about the class?"
- The teachers talk shop about the class. This includes descriptions of observations or hypotheses about the learners' styles of learning as well as storytelling about the learners (usually by the teacher).
- The leader facilitates a short closure during which procedural items are discussed (e.g., setting a date and time for the next observation, assigning tasks to be completed before the next meeting).
- Do you think these group procedures would be useful for your teacher development group? If not, why not?
- Come up with other effective procedures.

The question of leadership is very important for groups that want to provide as many opportunities as possible for each member to participate in the discussions. A more suitable name for this leader would be *facilitator*. Group members are encouraged to express their views in order to meet their own learning needs—to reflect on their work. A good facilitator will encourage discussion and support the group in developing a routine of open discussion. As Lieberman and Grolnick (1998) point out, teacher groups play a major role in "providing opportunities for teachers to validate both teacher knowledge and teacher inquiry" (p. 723).

Reflection Break 41
Group Leader or Facilitator

Many factors are involved in choosing a leader. Consider the following:

- Rules must be established for the role of the leader. What are the leader's responsibilities? What are the leader's powers (e.g., to decide on a topic, end a topic, nominate speakers, etc.)?

(Continued)

(Continued)

- Are there any volunteers to be the leader? If there is more than one, the group should vote to select the leader.
- For groups with a volunteer leader, would the leader's responsibilities and powers differ from those of an elected leader? As a group, draw up a list of rules that includes answers to the questions posed.

If nobody wants to be the ongoing leader, then each meeting, a different member can take responsibility for deciding the location, topic, and rules of discussion and intervention.

Closely related to group leadership is the responsibility of setting and maintaining the topic to be discussed by the group. *Topic*, according to Speier (1973), is defined as an element of "conversational structure around which participants organize their concerted interactions" (p. 91). The person who controls the topic has the power to affect interaction within the group. This is done by "raising a topic," "shifting the topic," and finally "closing down a topic" (Speier, 1973). The participants should decide whether they want to stick rigidly to topics or to be flexible.

Reflection Break 42
Group Members' Roles and Responsibilities

What are your opinions on the following roles? See if you can add more roles.

The Participating Teachers' Roles:

- Sharing teaching experience
- Sharing reflections and insights on teaching
- Sharing struggles and joys in teaching
- Sharing struggles in understanding students' learning behaviors
- Generating possible research topics

The Facilitator-Leader's Roles:

- Setting the agenda

- Sharing areas of expertise as a teacher and an observer
- Acting as procedural leader, responsible for initiation, closure, changing topics, and research-related topics.

Teacher Groups: Some Cautions

Recently, one U.S. university researcher and eight high school teachers came together as a group, initiated by the researcher, to reflect on their work (Nieto et al., 2002). They met once a month, for two hours, in a high school where one of the teachers worked. They talked about books they read together and discussed the daily challenges faced by many teachers in their classrooms. Some of the teachers brought their students' work to share with the group. Occasionally, they would E-mail each other. As the group's agenda slowly began to take shape over the year, they decided that each teacher would share his or her particular dilemma, focusing on obstacles that impeded their students' learning.

Although the group participants all agreed that the discussions were "inspiring, thought-provoking and disquieting" (Nieto et al., p. 352), they also admitted that the group raised more questions than it answered. They did, however, note that in today's educational climate of educational reform, fewer teachers than ever are motivated to remain in the teaching profession. They suggested that teachers need to be treated as "entire human beings, as professionals and intellectuals who care deeply about their students and their craft" (p. 352). Reflecting on practice with a group of teachers can help humanize teaching so that frustrations, dilemmas, joys, failures and successes, methods, and much more can be meaningfully shared with colleagues.

Reflection Break 43
Setting Up a Teacher Development Group

Now that you have read and reflected on the various aspects and issues related to reflective pairs or groups of teachers, it is time

(Continued)

(Continued)

to start putting together your group. Think about and answer the following questions:

- What is the purpose of the group?
- How many members will the group consist of? (Pairs are possible, too.)
- What roles will each member have (including who will be the leader-facilitator)?
- Where will the group meet and how long should the meetings last?
- How will the group arrange for confidentiality?
- Will the group members engage in classroom observations (Chapter 7)?
- Will each member of the group keep a teaching journal (Chapter 8)?
- Will each member of the group compile a teaching portfolio (Chapter 9)?
- How will the group generate topics for reflection (Chapter 10)?

CHAPTER SEVEN

Classroom Observation to Aid Reflective Practice

W hen senior teachers, administrators, supervisors, and mentors mention that they are going to conduct classroom observations, the classroom teachers' responses (at least the teachers who are going to be observed) are often highly negative. It seems that many teachers (myself included)) go on the defensive when they hear that they are going to be observed while teaching. Unfortunately, the fear of the evaluative aspect of classroom observations can mask the possibility that they can be helpful.

Reflection Break 44
Classroom Observations: Delight or Despair?

When I conduct workshops on teacher development, I ask teachers the following question:

"How do you feel about having your class observed by another teacher or administrator?"

Here are two common responses:

1. Oh! I think it's great that my class is going to be observed. Now I can receive valuable feedback on my teaching that will help me grow as a teacher.

(Continued)

(Continued)

2. Oh, no! I hate being observed because I have this fear that my shortcomings will be exposed in some way.

   • How many teachers do you think respond with answer Number 1? Number 2? What would your answer be? Why?

If you chose the second answer in Reflection Break 44, you fall into the large group of teachers who fear classroom observations to the point of not being able to sleep the night preceding one. As one teacher explained to me before a classroom observation,

> I haven't had any experience of being watched. The observer keeps telling me that she is not going to judge me when she is in my class. But I feel fear. I had dreamed a bad dream about my class before I had the class that was to be observed. I don't want to think that this fear is from my inability.

Why do classroom observations evoke such negative feelings and emotions when, in fact, teachers are observed every day by their students? We may think that teachers should be used to being observed and should just get on with teaching. However, classroom observations often involve the observer giving judgments based on that observer's preconceived notions of what good teaching is or should be. This is probably the single most important reason for teachers going on the defensive: They perceive that they must defend what they are doing in their classrooms, rather than explain what they are doing in light of their planned pedagogical objectives.

This chapter discusses how classroom observations can be used to promote reflection rather than defensive, unproductive conversations. Observers are encouraged to use descriptions of teaching rather than making judgments about teaching. Ideally, classroom observations help teachers to make more informed choices about their teaching because others have helped them to better understand their own instructional processes.

**Reflection Break 45
Observing Classes**

- What feelings do you associate with classroom observations?
- Do you feel that you will get helpful feedback or worried that someone will evaluate and judge you (like the teacher quoted at the beginning of this chapter)?
- Have you ever been observed in the classroom? If yes, was it a positive or negative experience? If positive, why? If negative, why? Describe your experience.

CLASSROOM OBSERVATION: SELF

A teacher can carry out classroom observation alone, with another teacher (as in peer observation and critical friendships), or with a group of teachers. For teachers to "observe" their own teaching, they need to use equipment such as tape recorders or video recorders. Teachers may feel more comfortable starting with the use of a tape recorder rather than a video recorder; it is sometimes a shock to hear one's voice for the first time on tape, much less see oneself in action. The first time I recorded my voice on a tape recorder while teaching, I reacted by thinking, "Do I speak like that?" After recording your class for a while, you soon get used to hearing your own voice and can then move on to more insightful reflections. As you read on, you will learn about audio recording and video taping your classes and various ways these recordings can be used for reflecting on your practice (see the section "How Can Teachers Observe Classes?").

**Reflection Break 46
Self-Observation**

- Remind yourself to think about your teaching while you teach.

  Write down your thoughts on a piece of paper at various times during the lesson, if you get a chance.

  (*Continued*)

(Continued)

- Bring in a tape recorder. Even though we have not yet discussed what to do with the recordings, it will help you get used to listening to your class and help find the best place to put the recorder.

  Tape yourself teaching a number of classes.

  What is your reaction to hearing yourself talk in the classroom?

- Bring in a video camera.

  Tape yourself teaching a number of classes.

  What is your reaction to seeing *and* hearing yourself teach? What is your reaction to seeing your students in class?

- Make the following lists for both audio and video recording:

  What did you learn in terms of your teaching? Your students' learning?

  What did you learn about these methods of obtaining information about your class?

CLASSROOM OBSERVATION: PEERS AND CRITICAL FRIENDSHIPS

When teachers become more confident in observing their own classes with the use of technology, they may then want to share their findings with other teachers by discussing what they noted. Such discussion can lead to the initiation of peer observation. Of course, some teachers may want to skip the self-observation altogether and jump right into finding peers willing to observe them and offer feedback. But peer observation is not always possible, as it involves establishing a high level of trust with another teacher. Also, certain rules must be established before commencing the observations, such as defining the role of the observer, determining the number of observations to be conducted, and deciding if both teachers will have their classes observed.

Reflection Break 47
Observation and Critical Friendships

- Ask a friend or colleague to join you in a critical friendship.
- Draw up a list of observation rules that both observers should follow when you conduct classroom observations.
- Ask your critical friend to observe you teach *without* giving any feedback. This will get you used to having a peer in your room.
- Observe your friend's teaching, if invited.
- Meet and discuss your feelings associated with having a peer observe while you teach.

Read the next sections in the text on how to observe and what to do with the recordings before conducting further observations.

The Purpose of Observation

Why would teachers want to conduct observations of their classes? Use Reflection Break 48 to think about some reasons why you would want to observe or have your class observed.

Reflection Break 48
Purpose of Observation

- Why would a teacher want to have his or her class observed?
- What might be the benefits of classroom observation?
- What can a teacher learn from being observed by a peer?
- What topics would you like to address in a classroom observation?

Reasons to observe might include the following:

- To become more aware of what you actually do in class
- To become more aware of what other teachers do in class

- To compare what you actually do in class with your beliefs about what you should be doing
- To get feedback from a peer

Reflection Break 49
Classroom Observations and Awareness

Good and Brophy (1991, pp. 26-27) have outlined the following six classroom problems that resulted from lack of teacher awareness of their own behaviors in the classroom:

1. Teacher domination

2. Overuse of factual questions

3. Few attempts to motivate students

4. Unawareness of effects of seat location and grouping

5. Overreliance on repetitive seatwork

6. Lack of emphasis on meaning

Now consider the following:

- Have you ever experienced any of these problems in your teaching? If yes, explain what happened and how you reacted.
- Think of other problems that could occur in the classroom if teachers are unaware of their behavior and actions in the classroom.

There are many reasons why teachers are unaware of what happens in their classrooms. So much takes place so quickly that a teacher cannot hope to see and monitor everything that goes on. This is where technology (audio recordings and video recordings) can help. Having an outside observer can give the teacher another eye on classroom events. Another reason teachers are unaware of what is happening in classrooms is that teacher education programs have not equipped them with the skills for analyzing classroom behavior, and they may not have the necessary terminology to discuss the teaching process. However, by becoming more aware of their teaching behaviors by conducting classroom observations, teachers can help narrow any gaps between their beliefs about what they are doing in the classroom and what they actually do.

How Can Teachers Observe Classes?

There are several ways teachers can approach classroom observation. I take both qualitative and quantitative approaches to observation, typically favoring qualitative. For suggestions on practicing a quantitative approach, see Reflection Breaks 53, 54, and 55 at the end of the chapter.

Using a qualitative point of view means looking at a classroom from many different angles, then putting all the information together at the end to see what picture has been painted. To do this, teachers must gather data from audio or video recordings or both, by sitting in on and observing a class while taking ethnographic notes (describing what happens as it happens), and by asking the observed teacher for thoughts on how the class went. This information is then mixed with the overall picture of the classroom, the students, their backgrounds, the teacher and his or her background, and the context within the school and the wider community.

Reflection Break 50
Audio and Video Recordings

- Have you ever audio recorded your classes? If yes,

  What was your reaction to hearing your own voice and the voices of your students?

  Did you have any problems with where you placed the audio recorder? If so, what were they?

- Have you ever videotaped your classes? If yes,

  What was your reaction to seeing yourself teaching for the first time?

(Continued)

(Continued)

> Did you have any problems with where you placed the video recorder? If so, what were they?
>
> How did the students react to the video recorder in the classroom? Were they comfortable being recorded?
>
> How did you react to having a video camera in the room while you taught? Did you alter your teaching?

- Do you think the video camera should be focused on the teacher or the students (assuming you have only one camera at your disposal)? Where would you place the camera and why?

Audio and Video Recordings

Teachers may want to start with audio recording their classes before videotaping, as audio-recorded classes may be less threatening, for both them and their students. When teachers have gotten used to hearing their own voices while teaching and have practiced transcribing what they hear, they may be ready to move on to videotaping. Both teacher and students may need some time to get used to having a video camera in the classroom and, for this reason, teachers should place a video camera in each class for a significant period of time (about two weeks) so that all are used to having the camera present.

If teachers and students do not get comfortable with the camera, the data gathered could be heavily influenced by the ripple effect (i.e., when a stone is thrown in water, it produces ripples; when an observer, tape recorder, or video camera is present in class, it too affects the flow of the lesson). We can never get rid of the ripple effect entirely, but we can minimize it by giving the class time to get used to being observed, mechanically or otherwise.

When teachers use audio and video recordings of their classes to learn about their teaching, they have to make some choices about how they will analyze what they see and hear.

Reflection Break 51
Using Audio and Video Recordings

- What should teachers do with audio and video recordings of their classes?
- Is it enough just to listen to an audio recording of your class? Why or why not?
- Is it enough to watch the videotape of your class? Why or why not?
- Should teachers transcribe all of the class or only parts? Why or why not?
- How long do you think it takes to transcribe a one-hour class? (It takes me about eight hours.)

Audio and videotapes have one advantage over the classroom observer: They can be watched or listened to as often as a teacher desires. Teachers can transcribe all or parts of a tape (both audio and video). If teachers have a direct focus and reason for the classroom observation (such as an examination of the type of questions they ask), they can transcribe the relevant parts only (such as every time the teacher asks a question). However, by transcribing all of a class, teachers can have a better chance of observing patterns in their teaching. This will help them effectively explore all aspects of their teaching. Later, they can focus in and conduct action research projects on particular aspects of their teaching.

Reflection Break 52
Focus of Classroom Observations

- On which topics would you like to focus your classroom observation? List these topics in order of importance to you. Examples could include the following:

    Where do I look when I am teaching my class (use of video: the teacher's action zone)?

(Continued)

(Continued)

How do I begin and end my classes (audio and video)?

How do I give instructions (audio and video)?

How do I give feedback (audio and video)?

• Think of some more.

Once teachers have collected information about their teaching, they may wonder what to do next. It is all well and good to receive feedback, but what does it mean? How can teachers analyze and interpret what has happened and why? The final step is for the teacher to consider whether or not to continue teaching in the same way. If the teacher is analyzing an audio recording, it may be too time-consuming to transcribe all of the tape, as it takes quite some time to transcribe one hour of class. Depending on their focuses, teachers can transcribe short sections by taking notes while listening to the tape. If the teacher is analyzing a video recording with a peer, they can play the video and stop at sections they think important, replaying events that happened in the class.

Next, the teachers should reflect on what happened and analyze the events they found most interesting. They can do this by asking themselves and their peer observers questions such as, "Why do I teach this way?" or "Do my beliefs and classroom practices align?" By seeking answers to these questions, teachers can challenge themselves (or be challenged by peers) to become reflective and obtain greater awareness about what they do. After some self-analysis, they can decide if they want to continue to teach as they do, or change. Change does not necessarily mean the implementation of certain teaching behavior modifications; change can also mean increased awareness about what they are doing and being comfortable with it.

Some educators have cautioned that a qualitative approach to classroom observation may be too broad a form of analysis for four reasons:

1. It does not address specific questions.

2. It is difficult to compare results with other classes.

3. It requires a highly trained observer to be able to keep up with and record all of the dynamic action within a classroom.

4. Whatever the observer records will be biased toward what he or she thinks important.

If teachers are uncomfortable with qualitative observations, they can conduct more quantitative observations by using tally sheets and checklists. The following three reflective breaks give examples of questions with more measurable answers that teachers can use before, during, and after lessons to help reflect on them.

Reflection Break 53
Lesson Planning Before Class

Teachers should answer the following questions, to plan what they would like to achieve in their lessons:

- What do you want the students to learn and why?
- What activities will you use to achieve those learning objectives?
- Are you going to "teach" a skill or "test" it? If testing, what teaching have you carried out before that you are now testing?
- Which materials or aids will you use in class and why?
- How will you check your students' understanding of the different stages of the lesson?
- How will you monitor each individual student's understanding of the lesson?
- How will you begin and end the lesson?

Think of other questions teachers can reflect on before class.

For further clarification of the success of a lesson, teachers could ask students at the end of each class to share their opinions about the lesson. The answers to these questions can assist teachers with future lesson planning.

**Reflection Break 54
After the Lesson**

The following questions may be useful for teachers to reflect on after conducting a lesson. Answers can be used as a basis for future lesson planning:

- What do you think the students actually learned?
- Which tasks were most successful? Least successful? Why?
- Did you finish the lesson on time?
- What changes (if any) will you make in your teaching and why or why not?
- What was the tempo of the lesson—fast or slow?
- Was it an appropriate tempo for what you were trying to achieve in the lesson?
- Is your answer to the previous question related to the activities you had set up: some to encourage learners to use their initiative, and others in which the students had to follow the teacher?
- Were the students active or passive?

Think of other questions teachers can reflect on after the lesson.

This chapter has demonstrated how teachers can become more reflective practitioners by conducting classroom observations. Classroom observation is a learned activity, and teachers' expertise can improve with practice. In addition, by conducting classroom observations, teachers can take more responsibility for their own professional development; they can make decisions based on what they know they currently do as teachers and what they would like to do in the future. In this age of accountability in education, teachers can make a better case for directing their own professional development by knowing exactly what goes on in their own classrooms and what other teachers are doing in theirs.

Reflection Break 55
Evaluating Lesson Effectiveness

Consider asking students the following questions to evaluate the effectiveness of a lesson:

- What do you think today's lesson was about?
- Which part was easiest?
- Which part was most difficult?
- What changes would you suggest that I make?

What other questions can teachers ask students to judge the effectiveness of a given lesson.

CHAPTER EIGHT

Journal Writing to Aid Reflective Practice

Reflective practice means taking the time to think about what we do as teachers. We can reflect simply by questioning ourselves about our work, by talking to other teachers about teaching (see Chapter 6), and by observing our classes (see Chapter 7). This chapter outlines another method we can use to reflect on our work: writing about it in a diary or journal. Writing about teaching in a diary or journal can help organize our thoughts into more systematic reflections about our work, especially if the journal writing is linked to other reflective activities, such as group discussions and classroom observations. By writing about our group discussions and classroom observations and looking for patterns from these activities, we can obtain more insight into who we are as teachers, allowing us to make more informed choices about our teaching.

Regularly writing in a journal can be a cathartic experience, especially if the journal is used to let off steam about frustrations encountered during the teaching day. It is also advisable to write about our successes in the classroom. By writing about what went wrong and what went well, we can look for patterns in both to understand why we perceived these classroom events as successful or not. This kind of analysis leads to further reflection on the beliefs we bring into the classroom and how we teach with or without them in mind, as the case may be. A teaching journal is a tool for us to use to explore our teaching beliefs and practices. As such, journals help us to be more systematic in our reflections.

> ### Reflection Break 56
> ### Writing About Teaching
>
> - Have you ever written any kind of diary or journal? If so, what kind of experiences did you write about?
> - Have you ever written a journal exclusively about teaching? If so, what kind of experiences did you write about?
> - If you have never written any kind of diary or journal, do you think it would be useful for a teacher (or student) to write a journal? If so, what kind of entries would you expect to find in such a journal?

KEEPING TEACHING JOURNALS

Make writing a social activity. It does not have to be an isolated act in which we lock ourselves away in a room. Marcel Proust (as quoted in Rodby, 1990) may have viewed writing as a "secretion of one's innermost self, done in solitude, for one's self alone" (p. 42), but he does not speak for all. In teaching journals, we are in actuality *interacting* with the text, as we can "see" in writing what we are thinking.

Writing is a process of discovery for the writer. By writing down our thoughts about a topic, we come to know ourselves better, allowing us to shape and reshape ourselves. Over time we can see patterns emerge in the writing. By recognizing and responding to these patterns, we grow and develop professionally. We may then choose to share our writing with other teachers to make the social cycle complete. Keeping a teaching journal can be as easy or complex an activity as we want: from simply writing about what happened during class to a more systematic analysis of what happened and why, as in an actual diary study.

Why Keep a Teaching Journal?

First, take a look at Reflection Break 57.

Reflection Break 57
Why Keep a Teaching Journal?

- List as many reasons as you can for wanting to write about your teaching.
- Would you share your writing with other teachers? Why or why not?

By writing in a teaching journal, we freeze our work so that we can reflect deliberately on it. Holly (1989) has pointed out that reflective journal writing can give us time to think about our work "long enough to reflect on it and to begin to understand it" (p. 78). Writing can be used to collect data about topics we want to reflect on in the form of an action research project. Journal writing can also help us look for patterns in our teaching over time. By discovering these patterns, we can find areas of our work we may need to change, or we may discover that we are happy with what we have been doing in the classroom. The point is that we can become more aware of what we are doing by writing about it.

Through different forms of journal writing—individual writing and writing for a peer or group—teachers can step back from their experiences and reflect on them. By analyzing these experiences, teachers give interpretation and meaning to the events and emotions they have chosen to document. In addition, journal writing can be an activity for teachers to collaborate with one another on projects such as action research projects, new innovations in teaching, and opinions of new curriculum initiatives.

How Can I Start a Teaching Journal?

Consider the questions in Reflection Break 58 before actually beginning a teaching journal.

Reflection Break 58
Starting Your Journal

Now would be a good time to begin your teaching journal. To start, you must consider the following questions:

- Will you use a computer or an ordinary notebook?
- Will you organize your writing or will you just free write your thoughts and rearrange them later?
- Who is your audience: yourself, a peer, a group, or an instructor?
- What will you focus your writing on: a lesson, a technique or method, a theory, a question posed, or some aspect of your job outside of the classroom?
- How regularly will you write: after a lesson, once a day, or once a week?
- How regularly will you review what you have written: every one, two, or three weeks?

The questions posed in Reflection Break 58 are all very important for each teacher to consider before actually beginning the act of writing. For example, some teachers may want to write their journal entries in a notebook after each class, while others may prefer to word process at the end of each day or during the week for a specific period of time. Teachers must make these decisions based on their individual writing objectives and preferred styles.

A teaching journal can be written alone in the form of a diary for private use, not to be shared. Journals can also be written as part of a critical friendship (see Chapter 6), writing to and for each other, or in a group, writing to and for each other. In addition, teachers can collaborate on writing journal entries if they want to share constructing the actual journal as an interactive group (like writing a group essay). In this technological age, journal writing can be done on a computer word processing program (individual) and shared through E-mail. Last, teachers can speak or talk their journal entries into a tape recorder for later analysis. The teacher can decide whether to transcribe all or parts of the tape.

Reflection Break 59
Types of Teaching Journals

- Which of the following types of teaching journals appeals to you most?

  A hand-written notebook journal?

  A word-processed journal?

  A private journal?

  A journal with a critical friend?

  An electronic mail (E-mail) journal with a peer or group?

  A group journal constructed as a group?

  A spoken journal (audio recorded)?

- Think of another type or format of teaching journal.

The main goal is to write about teaching experiences as regularly as possible over a period of time and then to analyze the entries for patterns and insights. Alternatively, the teaching journals need not be analyzed. If they are not analyzed, then they serve as a history of what the teacher is doing and has done.

When teachers are both the writers and the audiences of the journals, they should not worry about spelling, grammar, style, or organization. They should just free write about whatever issues are important for them within their work. However, to make these journal entries meaningful, they should be examined after some time and analyzed for recurring patterns of events or themes. This way, teachers can become more aware of themselves; their teaching behaviors; their students; and their beliefs, values, and practices.

Teachers can also write for other teachers so that they get feedback, as in critical friendships or with a group of teachers. In critical friendships, this collaboration offers opportunities for teachers to support and, at times, challenge each other, along with evidence from classroom observations. This type of journal may require more formal entries, in that the organization (and grammar) must be clear to another reader. It is the writer's responsibility to make the entries clear, not the reader's responsibility to have to make interpretations about what the writer may be trying to say. Teachers must also decide if they want the reader(s) to make comments about what was written (orally or in writing—E-mail communications are good for this).

Reflection Break 60
Finding a Focus for Your Writing

This activity will help to focus your writing.

- Write a journal entry for yourself, a peer or critical friend, or a group using the following guidelines:

  Focus on a recent issue you found important in your teaching or an actual problem you encountered in your teaching.

  Now analyze that problem in light of your beliefs about teaching and learning.

  Interpret what you have found (if you are writing for a critical friend or a group, ask them for feedback on the analysis and interpretation phases).

  Last, ask yourself what all this means to you as a teacher. Do you need to change anything?

- Do you think the foregoing format for formal journal writing is helpful or not? Explain.

Teaching journals that require other teachers to read them usually require the audience to respond to the author.

Reflection Break 61
Responding to Journals

- If you write a journal for a peer, what type of response would you like to see from him or her?
- Would you like the reader to challenge you? Why?
- Would you like the reader to make judgments or not?
- Would you like the responses orally or in writing? Why?

(Continued)

(Continued)

- Would you respond to the feedback you'd received?
- What cautions would you give a peer about how to respond to a teacher's journal?

Make up a list of rules about how teachers should respond to each other's journals.

I cannot say how teachers should respond to another teacher's journal, as each entry will most likely be specific to the context. However, I would suggest that each teacher use nonjudgmental and supportive language when writing a response to a journal entry.

Writing Topics—Examples

Experienced teachers may use a teaching journal for concerns such as how to keep students working while also controlling discipline in the room. For example, I used teaching journals with a group of experienced language teachers (Farrell, 1998) and discovered that these teachers wrote about similar topics over a sixteen-week period. The most frequent topic in their journals related to their approaches to and methods of teaching (fifty-six references), followed by evaluations of their teaching (forty-nine references), their theories of teaching (thirty-nine references), their levels of self-awareness (fifteen references), and various questions they raised about teaching (five references).

The teachers wrote most frequently about their methods of teaching, the procedures they use in their classrooms, and the content of their lessons. They rarely wrote about the theories underlying these approaches and methods. Their source of knowledge was mostly traced to their classroom experience. Although they mentioned their students in broader school contexts, the major focus remained in their classroom experiences. The teachers evaluated their teaching more negatively than positively and primarily in terms of the problems that occurred. They generated few solutions of their own.

On the topic of theories and beliefs, the teachers wrote about their personal beliefs (personal opinions) and justifications. There were no references to actual theories of teaching or learning. The last two categories consisted of references to perceptions of themselves as teachers and the infrequent asking of questions seeking advice. What was striking about all these entries was that the teachers never wrote about the successes or joys of teaching. In fact, they saw the teaching journal primarily as a place to let off steam.

Reflection Break 62
Topics to Consider Writing About

As mentioned in the text, experienced teachers in the reflective journal writing study wrote about the following topics (in order of most frequent references):

1. Approaches to and methods of teaching

2. Evaluations of their teaching

3. Theories of teaching

4. Self-awareness as a teacher

5. Questions about teaching

Now consider the following:

- Which of the foregoing five topics would you write about in a teaching journal? Why?
- Think of other topics to write about in teaching.

A teaching journal records what happens in a teacher's life, both inside and outside of the classroom. Teachers should revisit these events later to make sense of them so that they can better understand themselves as teachers. Interpretations based on patterns noticed in these journals will help teachers make more informed decisions about their work. Keeping a journal can also be a first step in compiling a teaching portfolio, which will be discussed in the next chapter.

Reflection Break 63
Reflecting on Practice

Here are some questions that teachers can consider answering. in their journals as a means of reflecting on practice from a general point of view. Rather than focusing on a particular problem or issue, look at teaching from a broad perspective. Teachers may want to use the feedback from classroom observations to help them answer these questions. When teachers have written answers to these questions, they can share with other teachers in order to get more feedback.

- Describe what you do, without judgment.
- Why do you do it?
- What do others do?
- What was the result?
- Should you continue to do this or change it?
- What change will you make?

CHAPTER NINE

Creating a Teaching Portfolio to Aid Reflective Practice

U sing portfolios as a means of assessment is not a new concept. However, it is only recently that portfolios have become popular in teacher education and development programs. A teaching portfolio is a collection of information about a teacher's practice. A teaching portfolio also provides a means for reflecting on and critiquing one's work. According to Costantino and De Lorenzo (2002), teachers who compile teaching portfolios take more responsibility for their development. As a result, "The process of reflecting and documenting what they know and are able to do is highly empowering and contributes to [a teacher's] self-confidence" (p. 5).

Reflection Break 64
A Teaching Portfolio

- Have you ever compiled a portfolio of any kind? If yes, please explain what kind of portfolio you compiled and your reasons for compiling it.
- Have you ever compiled a *teaching* portfolio? If yes, please explain what kind of portfolio you compiled and your reasons for compiling it.

TEACHING PORTFOLIOS

A teaching portfolio is an album, much like a photo album, containing many aspects of a teacher's work. It tells the story of the teacher's efforts, skills, abilities, achievements, and contributions to students, colleagues, institutions, academic disciplines, and community. Evans (1995) defines a teaching portfolio in the following way: "A professional portfolio is an evolving collection of carefully selected or composed professional thoughts, goals and experiences that are threaded with reflection and self-assessment" (p. 11).

A teaching portfolio might include (but is not limited to) lesson plans, anecdotal records, student projects, class newsletters, videotapes, annual evaluations, and letters of recommendation. It should be remembered that the teaching portfolio is not a one-time snapshot of where the teacher is at present; it is a growing collection of carefully selected and recorded professional experiences, thoughts, and goals. After collecting and assembling all the materials for their teaching portfolios, teachers must reflect on what they have put together and assess their current and future teaching plans.

Reflection Break 65
Contents of a Teaching Portfolio

Possible contents of a teaching portfolio include the following items: lesson plans, student projects, class newsletters, videotapes, annual evaluations, and letters of recommendation.

- How long would it take you to compile the components of a teaching portfolio?
- Can you think of any other items that you could include in your portfolio that tell the story of your efforts and skills as a teacher? List them.
- Include the contents of your group discussions (Chapter 6), classroom observations (Chapter 7), and journal writing (Chapter 8) in your teaching portfolio.

Why Compile a Teaching Portfolio?

Two words should be enough to convince you to begin a teaching portfolio: *reflection* and *direction*. As a reflective device, a portfolio offers teachers the chance to get truly good looks at themselves, as if looking into a mirror. It literally allows teachers to see how they have evolved over time. After reviewing the evidence collected over time, teachers can reflect on where they were, where they currently are, and most important, where they want to go. As a source of direction, a portfolio is a starting point for further development, as the teacher creates a plan for the future and sets goals.

Reflection Break 66
Portfolios for Reflection and Direction

- Briefly describe what *reflection* and *direction* mean to you in terms of compiling a teaching portfolio.
- What images or items do you have that you might like to include in a teaching portfolio?
- What direction would you like to take professionally as a teacher? (Think about this before you start your teaching portfolio)

The most beneficial aspect of compiling a teaching portfolio is that it cultivates reflection and self-assessment (Evans, 1995). The process of portfolio development requires answers to the following questions, some familiar, some new:

- Who are you as a teacher?
- What do you do in the classroom (and outside that is related to teaching)?
- Why do you do it?
- Where do you want to go in your teaching?
- How do you plan to get there?

To answer these questions, teachers must research their own practices.

Reflection Break 67
Artifacts That Represent You as a Teacher

- What artifacts (objects) best represent what you do as a teacher?
- Review the reflection exercises and your reactions and answers to the exercises in the first eight chapters of this book.

How might you include the insights you have gained from the Reflection Breaks in your teaching portfolio?

Types of Teaching Portfolios

There are three main types of portfolios (Costantino & De Lorenzo, 2002) that practicing teachers can compile:

The Working Portfolio

Teachers use a working portfolio to document growth and development toward performance standards that may have been set within the institution, the state, or at the national level. The materials included in this portfolio are intended to reflect work in progress and growth over time; they are not intended to be polished documents.

The Showcase Portfolio

Teachers use this portfolio to literally showcase a collection of exemplary documents and artifacts that highlight their best work and accomplishments. Teachers can use showcase portfolios to share information about themselves with colleagues and administrators. They can also be presented to employers when pursuing promotion and for seeking further employment.

The Critical Incident Portfolio

Teachers use critical incident portfolios to document events they found to be particularly provocative and illuminating. Teachers should include captions that explain the rationale for choosing the topics and reflective statements about the critical incidents. In this way, teachers can outline their underlying philosophy of teaching and learning.

Collecting Documents for Teaching Portfolios

There are many materials and documents a teacher can choose to include, but having too many documents can present a difficult task for the reviewer. Only those documents that are critical to the purpose of the portfolio should be chosen. A good rule of thumb is to place the most recent artifacts at the beginning of the portfolio.

Any teaching portfolio, regardless of the specific purpose for creating it, should always include items that document the following:

- Knowledge of subject matter
- The manner of planning, delivering, and assessing instruction
- Professionalism

Knowledge of Subject Matter

This first section of the teaching journal should outline what you know about the subject you teach and how it impacts your classroom. Documents that demonstrate your knowledge of the subject matter might include the following materials:

- Highlights of a unit of instruction, reflections on the class, and implications for future instruction
- A research paper (or other original materials such as books, papers, etc.) you have written on the subject you teach and what you learned from the contents of the paper as it relates to your teaching (showing that you are reflecting on the subject matter you teach)
- Descriptions of courses or workshops you have conducted
- A reflective journal you have been keeping about your teaching of the subject matter
- A reflective essay about how your knowledge of the subject matter has informed your instructional decisions and how you plan to increase student learning

Reflection Break 68
Looking Back at Journal Writing

- Quickly review Chapter 8 (Journal Writing).

  Find any documents that you have written as a result of the Reflection Breaks that you can include in this section of your teaching portfolio.

- Include any other information garnered from the Reflective Breaks in the earlier chapters of this book.

Planning, Delivering, and Assessing Instruction

This section of the portfolio reflects who you are as a teacher. Documents for this section include the following:

- A written reflection of your beliefs about teaching and learning
- Sample lesson plans
- Samples of student work
- Samples of students' evaluations and feedback regarding your lessons
- A videotape or audiotape (or both) of you teaching a class, with a written description of what you were teaching and your reflections about that class
- Feedback from a supervisor or an administrator
- Classroom observation report from a peer teacher

Reflection Break 69
Looking Back at Classroom Observations

- Take another look at Chapter 7 (Classroom Observations). See if there is any information you discovered about your teaching that you can include in the Planning section of your teaching portfolio.
- Include any other information garnered from the Reflection Breaks in the earlier chapters of this book.

Professionalism

The final section of the teaching portfolio demonstrates who you are as a teacher in the wider community. Your professionalism is viewed in terms of activities and contributions to organizations, students, teachers, and parents. Documents that can be compiled for this section include the following:

- A current professional development plan, including action steps
- A current resume
- A list of memberships in professional organizations
- A description of any leadership positions held, such as head of department, curriculum development unit, and committees (including student and parent)
- Copies of degrees, certificates, honors, and awards held

Reflection Break 70
Your Professional Development Plan

- Write out a professional development plan that includes what and how you will continue to reflect on your teaching.
- Update your current resume for this section of the teaching portfolio.

Now it is time to compile your teaching portfolio. Remember, take your time; don't try to put it all together in one day.

Reflection Break 71
Compiling Your Teaching Portfolio

Now that you know about the three main sections of a teaching portfolio (knowledge of subject matter; planning, delivering, and assessing instruction; and professionalism), it is time for you to compile your own portfolio.

(Continued)

(Continued)

- Compile your working portfolio first, and then move into a showcase portfolio.
- Once you have finished your showcase portfolio, begin working on your critical incident portfolio.

To recap, teaching portfolios can provide teachers with opportunities for self-reflection and collaboration with colleagues in addition to opportunities to plan individual professional development paths. The analogy of taking a journey is applicable to preparing teaching portfolios. Just as travellers must decide their points of departure, the courses they will take, and their destinations, teachers must think about their starting points, directions, and goals for the coming years in compiling their portfolios.

Reflection Break 72
Reflecting on Your Teaching Portfolio

- Now that you have compiled a showcase teaching portfolio, reflect on its contents and how this portfolio represents you as a teacher.
- Find another teacher who has also compiled a teaching portfolio and give each other feedback on them.

CHAPTER TEN

Generating Topics for Reflection

I t is common that experienced teachers do not readily talk about their teaching outside of official staff meetings. As a result, individual experiences are not often shared informally. However, it is important that veteran teachers share their stories and knowledge with novices, who would certainly benefit from such discussions. One way to open the door of communication is to have individual teachers or a group of teachers generate their own reflective topics. This chapter proposes four methods that can be used to stimulate thinking about teaching topics to reflect on. All four activities assume that the participants are open-minded, responsible teachers and that they will wholeheartedly engage in each activity so that they can get to know themselves better as teachers.

Generating Topics for Reflection

Generating topics for reflection is the most involved of the four activities presented in this chapter. The purpose of this activity is to show teachers that they can certainly come up with their own topics (in the form of teaching dilemmas or teaching successes), and they can also become more aware of what these topics mean in the bigger picture of their teaching beliefs and practices. This activity can be embarked upon by an individual teacher reflecting alone; however, that teacher will not receive any feedback on any of the various steps of the activity. It is best if a group of teachers engages in the activity together—the more the better. For example, one department in the school can come together to reflect on particular dilemmas the teachers perceive to be important. Together, they can brainstorm potential solutions to the challenges they face.

Reflection Break 73
Generating Topics for Reflection

Teachers should individually answer the following question (pairs and groups come together later):

- Reflect on a recent teaching practice you tried or an experience that happened in your classroom that caused you to stop and think about your teaching.

It is best to write ideas and answers on a piece of paper to facilitate sharing with the other members of the group.

- Have each teacher share his or her answer to the question posed in Reflection Break 73 with group members. If there is a large number of teachers, groups of four or five participants can be set up. Each teacher should also explain why he or she chose a particular topic to reflect on.
- Group members can then see if there are any similarities among the topics chosen and, if so, combine similar topics into one. If there are no similar topics, then group members should rank the topics in the order they deem most important.

Reflection Break 74
Sample Topics for Reflection

Here are eight examples of topics that teachers have considered important, taken from workshops that I have conducted:

1. Helping students to think on their own

2. Motivating students

3. Maintaining interest and attention in diverse groups

4. Getting control of elementary school students

5. Effectively teaching to large classes

6. Ensuring student progress

7. Improving teacher confidence

8. Making informed decisions

Now answer this question:

- Do you consider these topics relevant and important to you as a teacher? Why or why not?
- Suggest other valuable topics for reflection.

- Group members can list topics on the board and generate possible solutions to each topic in turn. If there is more than one group, then all groups can share their topics together. If there are too many topics to discuss, remedy the dilemma by first having the group as a whole write all of the topics on the board and then decide collectively which two or three topics to focus on during that particular group meeting. The other topics can be addressed at subsequent meetings.

Reflection Break 75
Generating Solutions

Here are some examples of responses to four challenges identified by teachers who participated in workshops I conducted:

1. Large classes (fifty or more students):

   Do group or pair work whenever possible.

2. Ensuring student progress:

   Teachers should have sound methods of assessment and give lots of feedback.

3. Lack of student motivation:

   Topics must have relevance to students' lives and experiences.

(Continued)

(Continued)

4. Improving teacher confidence:

   Confident teachers have more opportunities for professional advancement.

Now answer this question:

- Do you consider these topics relevant and important to you as a teacher? Why or why not?
- Suggest other topics you consider important to reflect on.

Encourage participants to suggest solutions to each of the ranked topics, depending on time available.

For teachers wishing to conduct similar workshops in different contexts, it is important to remember that the participants must be advised to take an active role in all the activities. Sixty minutes should be enough time to complete the workshop.

What Is Your Conception of Teaching?

This section can be seen as a mini-workshop asking you to look at your conceptions of teaching (from Freeman & Richards, 1993). To do this, you should determine which aspects of Freeman and Richards's tripartite classification system fit your style. It is possible to place yourself within all three of the categories.

The Tripartite Classification of Conceptions of Teaching is as follows:

- Science and Research Conception
- Theory and Values Conception
- Art and Craft Conceptions

Science and Research Conception

The science and research conception of teaching is derived from research and is supported by experimentation. Here, a tested model of learning informs teaching. This model contends that if teachers learn specific acts of teaching (such as effective questioning and effective wait time), then they will be good teachers. Teachers who employ a science and research conception of teaching record their classes or have others observe them, and they document their actions. For example, teachers who ground their practice in the science and research model would likely interpret high test scores as an indication of effective teaching.

Theory and Values Conception

This conception holds that teaching methods should be based on what *ought* to work or what is morally right to do. There is no empirical research to back up these conceptions of teaching. Reflective teaching and learner–centered teaching are examples of values–based approaches because teachers attach importance to them.

Art and Craft Conception

This conception recognizes that each teaching situation is different and unique. As a result, each teacher must decide how to teach, based on his or her individual personality and skill level. The teacher does not follow any one method and uses a range of teaching options.

Reflection Break 76
Conceptions of Teaching

Self-assess your conceptions of teaching:

- Reflect on each of the following conceptions of teaching. Circle the number you think best reflects the degree to which your teaching is influenced by that conception (1 = low; 5 = high).

CONCEPTION	ASSESSMENT				
➢ Science/Research	1	2	3	4	5
➢ Theory/Values	1	2	3	4	5
➢ Art/Craft	1	2	3	4	5

Life History

This next activity asks you to reflect on your personal journey as a teacher. I have put this activity near the end of the book rather than at the beginning because if you have attempted the activities in the previous chapters, you will already have completed a journey of sorts. You have also been reflecting on your teaching and your life as a teacher. Now you may be ready to reflect on the big picture, ready to tell your story as a teacher. According to Bullough (1997), telling one's story "is a way of getting a handle on what we believe, on models, metaphors and images that underpin action and enable meaning making, on our theories" (p. 19).

The life history activity in Reflection Break 77 asks you to examine some of the early influences in your life: where you were born, your family values, early experiences, and even your heritage. Next, examine your journey from childhood through high school and the influences that shaped you along the way. It is important for you to look for an experience (a critical incident) that modified or reshaped your view of teaching and yourself as a teacher (we will look at critical incidents in the next section). Last, look at where you are now in your career.

Reflection Break 77
Your Life History

- Briefly outline your life history:

  Your early experiences

  Your family life

  Your heritage

  Your religious background (if any)

  Your socioeconomic background

  Your regional background

  Your high school experiences

  Your college experiences (especially as a student teacher)

  Your first teaching experiences

> - List other experiences in your life that were important to you.
> - Describe any of those experiences you think may have significantly impacted your development as a teacher.

Critical Incidents in Teaching

According to Brookfield (1990), a critical incident is a "vividly remembered event" which is "unplanned and unanticipated" (p. 84). Teachers examine these incidents to understand their teaching and, ultimately, to improve it. Not all incidents that happen inside and outside of the classroom are critical for a teacher. As Tripp (1993) has observed, "incidents happen but critical incidents are produced by the way we look at a situation: a critical incident is an interpretation of a significant event" (p. 8). I will look at two types of critical incidents:

- Personal critical incidents: Events that occur during the course of a teacher's career
- Critical teaching incidents: Events that happen in the classroom related to the teaching

Personal Critical Incidents

This activity ties together teachers' life histories with their experiences of the teaching profession. A personal critical incident for a teacher is an event that resulted in a major change in the teacher's professional life. Think of yourself for a moment. Can you recall a specific circumstance or interaction that influenced you to become a teacher? Your Life History (see Refection Break 77) will give you an overall view of what has influenced your life. Your life history *as a teacher*—who you are, what has happened, and what you have done (see also Chapter 9: Teaching Portfolios)—can help you better understand your life in relation to your work. This knowledge may also help you figure out where you want to go as a teacher.

Reflection Break 78
Your Personal Critical Incidents

Look back at the Life History that you constructed in Reflection Break 77 and answer the following questions:

- What critical incidents in your youth shaped you as a teacher?
- What critical incidents during your college years shaped you as a teacher?
- What critical incidents in your early teaching days shaped you as a teacher?
- What general critical incidents in your career have shaped you as a teacher?
- Do you teach in reaction to any of these incidents? Explain.

Critical Teaching Incidents

Even though personal critical incidents have enormous consequences for teachers, the majority of critical incidents pertinent to teaching occur in their classrooms. These incidents are typically commonplace events to which teachers ascribe critical significance. To analyze these incidents they need to engage in reflective activities. A record of these can be kept by having their classrooms observed and by using technical recording equipment (see Chapter 7). Once the recorded information is transcribed and studied, teachers can effectively analyze critical incidents in the moment, thereby helping them understand why the incident had such a strong impact on their lives and their teaching practices. By writing in a teaching journal (see Chapter 8), teachers can also record the event, as well as their thoughts and feelings, soon after its occurrence.

Reflection Break 79
Your Critical Teaching Incidents

Review the critical incidents that you have documented in your teaching journal (see Chapter 8). Can you think of any others now? Choose one that happened in your class.

- Describe the incident.

  Why was this incident important to you?

  What was your reaction (if any) at the time of the incident?

  Did you stop teaching?

- What does this critical incident tell you about your beliefs and values as they relate to teaching?

Are You a Reflective Practitioner?

Now that you have completed reading this book, do you consider yourself a reflective practitioner? To help you answer this question, take a look at the final Reflection Break.

Reflection Break 80
Key Features of a Reflective Practitioner

Now that you have read some of the main issues surrounding reflective practice, it is time to identify some fundamental aspects of a reflective teacher.

Zeichner and Liston (1996, p. 6) have suggested five key features of a reflective teacher. Look at these features and assess how much you embody each of them. Write down your thoughts.

(Continued)

(Continued)

A reflective teacher:

1. Examines, frames, and attempts to solve dilemmas in classroom practice

2. Is aware of and questions the assumptions and values he or she brings to teaching

3. Is attentive to the institutional and cultural contexts in which he or she teaches

4. Takes part in curriculum development and is involved in school change efforts

5. Takes responsibility for his or her own professional development

Now go two steps farther:

- Give examples of each of these features from your recent reflections.
- Outline how you can incorporate each of these features into future reflections on your practice.

Bibliography

Acheson, K. A., & Gall, M. D. (1992). *Techniques in the clinical supervision of teachers* (3rd ed.). New York: Longman.

Alschuler, A. (1980). *Teacher burnout.* Washington, DC: National Education Association.

Argyris, C., & Schon, D. A. (1974). *Theory into practice.* New York: Jossey-Bass.

Bartlett, L. (1990). Teacher development through reflective teaching. In J. C. Richards & D. Nunan (Eds.), *Second language teacher education.* New York: Cambridge University Press.

Birchak, B., Connor, C., Crawford, K., Kahn, L., Kaser, S., Turner, S., & Short, K. (1998). *Teacher study groups.* Urbana, IL: National Council of Teachers of English.

Brookfield, S. (1990). *The skillful learner.* San Francisco: Jossey-Bass.

Brubacher, J. W., Case, C. W., & Reagan, T. G. (1994). *Becoming a reflective educator.* Thousand Oaks, CA: Corwin.

Buckley, J. (1999, July). *Multicultural reflection.* Paper presented at the annual meeting of the American Association of Colleges of Teacher Education, Washington, DC.

Bullough, R. V. (1997). Practicing theory and theorizing practice in teacher education. In J. Loughran & T. Russell (Eds.), *Teaching about teaching: Purpose, passion and pedagogy in teacher education* (pp. 13-31). London: Falmer.

Carr, W., & Kemmis, S. (1986). *Becoming critical: Education, knowledge and action research.* London: Falmer.

Clarke, A. (1995). Professional development in practicum settings: Reflective practice under scrutiny. *Teaching and Teacher Education, 11,* 243-261.

Cochran-Smith, M., and Lytle, S. (1993). *Inside/outside: Teacher research and knowledge.* New York: Teachers College Press.

Costantino, P., & De Lorenzo, M. (2002). *Developing a professional teaching portfolio.* Boston: Allyn & Bacon.

Cruickshank, D., & Applegate, J. (1981). Reflective teaching as a strategy for teacher growth. *Educational Leadership, 38*(7), 553-554.

Dana, N. F., & Yendol-Silva, D. (2003). *The reflective educator's guide to classroom research*. Thousand Oaks, CA: Corwin.

Day, C. (1993). Reflection: A necessary but not sufficient condition for teacher development. *British Educational Research Journal, 19*, 83-93.

Dewey, J. (1958). How we think. In W. B. Kolesnick, *Mental discipline in modern education*. Madison: University of Wisconsin Press. (Original work published in 1933)

Doyle, W., & Ponder, G. (1977-78). The ethic of practicality and teacher decision-making. *Interchange, 8*(3), 1-12.

Elbaz, F. (1988). Critical reflections on teaching: Insights from Freire. *Journal of Education for Teaching, 14*, 171-181.

Evans, S. M. (1995). *Professional portfolios: Documenting and presenting performance excellence*. Virginia Beach, VA: Teacher's Little Secrets.

Farrell, T. S. C. (1998). EFL teacher development through journal writing. *RELC Journal, 29*(1), 92-109.

Farrell, T. S. C. (1999). Reflective practice in an EFL development group. *System, 27*, 157-172.

Freeman, D., & Richards, J. C. (1993). Conceptions of teaching and the education of second language teachers. *TESOL Quarterly, 27*(2), 193-216.

Golby, M., & Appleby, R. (1995). Reflective practice through critical friendship: Some possibilities. *Cambridge Journal of Education 25*, 149-160.

Good, T. L., & Brophy, J. E. (1991). *Looking in classrooms* (5th ed.). New York: HarperCollins.

Goodman, J. (1984). Reflection and teacher education: A case study and theoretical analysis. *Interchange, 15*, 9-27.

Goodman, J. (1991). Using a methods course to promote reflection and inquiry among preservice teachers. In R. Tabachnick & K. Zeichner, (Eds.), *Issues and practices in inquiry-oriented teacher education*. London: Falmer.

Gore, J. (1987). Reflecting on reflective teaching. *Journal of Teacher Education, 38*(2), 33-39.

Hatton, N., & Smith, D. (1995). Reflection in teacher education: Towards definition and implementation. *Teaching and Teacher Education, 11*, 33-49.

Holly, D. (1989). Reflective writing and the spirit of inquiry. *Cambridge Journal of Education, 19*, 78-80.

Hoover, L. (1994). Reflective writing as a window on pre-service teachers' thought processes. *Teacher and Teacher Education, 10*, 83-93.

Jackson, P. (1968). *Life in classrooms*. New York: Holt.

James, P. (1996). Learning to reflect: A story of empowerment. *Teaching and Teacher Education, 12*, 81-97.

Jay, J. K., & Johnson, K. L. (2002). Capturing complexity: A typology of reflective practice for teacher education. *Teaching and Teacher Education, 18,* 73-85.

Killon, J., & Todnew, G. (1991). A process of personal theory building. *Educational Leadership, 48*(6), 14-16.

Korthagen, F. (1993). Two modes of reflection. *Teaching and Teacher Education, 9,* 317-326.

Ladson-Billings, G. (1999). Preparing teachers for diversity. In L. Darling-Hammond & G. Sykes (Ed.), *Teaching as the learning profession* (pp. 86-123). San Francisco: Jossey-Bass.

Lieberman, A., & Grolnick, M. (1998). Educational reform networks: Changes in the forms of reform. In A. Hargreaves, A. Lieberman, M. Fullan, & D. Hopkins (Eds.), *International handbook of educational change* (pp. 710-729). Boston: Kluwer.

McFee, G. (1993). Reflections on the nature of action-research. *Cambridge Journal of Education 23*(2), 173-183.

Nieto, S., Gordon, S., & Yearwood, J. (2002). Teachers' experiences in a critical inquiry group: A conversation in three voices. *Teaching Education, 13*(3), 341-355.

Oprandy, R., Golden, L., & Shiomi, K. (1999). Teachers talking about teaching: Collaborative conversations about an elementary ESL class. In J. Gebhard & R. Oprandy (Eds.). *Language teaching awareness.* New York: Cambridge University Press.

Parker, S. (1997). *Reflective teaching in the postmodern world: A manifesto for education in postmodernity.* Buckingham, UK: Open University Press.

Reiman, A. J. (1999). The evolution of the social roletaking and guided reflection framework in teacher education: Recent theory and quantitative synthesis of research. *Teaching and Teacher Education, 15,* 597-612.

Richert, A. E. (1991). Case methods and teacher education: Using cases to teach teacher reflection. In D. R. Tabachnick & K. M. Zeichner (Eds.), *Issues and practices in inquiry-oriented teacher education* (pp. 130–150). London: Falmer.

Rodby, J. (1990). The ESL writer and the kaleidoscopic self. *The Writing Instructor, 10,* 42-50.

Sagor, R. (1993). *How to conduct collaborative action research.* Alexandria, VA: Association for Supervision and Curriculum Development.

Schon, D. A. (1983). *The reflective practitioner.* New York: Basic Books.

Schon, D. A. (1990). *Educating the reflective practitioner: Towards a new design for teaching and learning in the profession.* San Francisco: Jossey-Bass.

Senge, P. M. (1990). *The fifth discipline.* New York: Currency & Doubleday.

Smyth, J. (1987). Developing and sustaining critical reflection in teacher education. *Journal of Teacher Education, 40*(2), 2-9.

Speier, M. (1973). *How to observe face-to-face communication: A sociological introduction.* Pacific Palisades, CA: Goodyear.

Taggart, G., & Wilson, A. P. (1998). *Promoting reflective thinking in teachers.* Thousand Oaks, CA: Corwin.

Tripp, D. (1993). *Critical incidents in teaching*: *Developing professional judgement.* London: Routledge.

Valli, L. (1999). Listening to other voices: A description of teacher reflection in the United States. *Peabody Journal of Education, 72*(1), 67–88.

Van Manen, M. (1977). Linking ways of knowing with ways of being practical. *Curriculum Inquiry, 6*, 205-228.

Van Manen, M. (1991). Reflectivity and the pedagogical moment: The normativity of pedagogical thinking and acting. *Journal of Curriculum Studies, 23*, 507-536.

Webb, P. T. (1999, April). *The use of language in reflective teaching: Implications for self-understanding.* Paper presented at the annual meeting of the American Educational Research Association, Montreal, Canada.

Zeichner, K. (1981). Reflective teaching and field-based experiences in teacher education. *Interchange, 12*, 1-22.

Zeichner, K., & Liston, D. P. (1987). Teaching student teachers to reflect. *HER, 57*(1), 22-48.

Zeichner, K. M., & Liston, D. P. (1996). *Reflective teaching: An introduction.* Mahwah, NJ: Lawrence Erlbaum.

Index

**CORWIN
PRESS**

The Corwin Press logo—a raven striding across an open book—represents the union of courage and learning. Corwin Press is committed to improving education for all learners by publishing books and other professional development resources for those serving the field of K–12 education. By providing practical, hands-on materials, Corwin Press continues to carry out the promise of its motto: "**Helping Educators Do Their Work Better**."